David Teniers the Younger

Jane P. Davidson

Westview Press / Boulder, Colorado

Copyright © 1979 by Westview Press, Inc.

Published in 1979 in the United States of America by
  Westview Press, Inc.
  5500 Central Avenue
  Boulder, Colorado 80301
  Frederick A. Praeger, Publisher

Library of Congress Cataloging in Publication Data
Davidson, Jane P.
  David Teniers the Younger.
  Bibliography: p.
  Includes index.
  1. Teniers, David, the Younger, 1610-1690. 2. Painters—Belgium—
  Biography. I. Title
ND673.T3D38   759.9493   [B]   79-13221
ISBN: 0-89158-564-8

Printed and bound in the United States of America

Contents

List of Plates

Preface

For some time there has existed a need for a new account of the life and stylistic development of David Teniers the Younger (1610-1690). This need is made all the more obvious by the fact that Adolf Rosenberg's book, written in 1898, remains a most complete study of Teniers.[1] De Peyre's *Biographie Critique* of 1910 added little information not already published by Rosenberg.[2] A number of recent articles have dealt with various aspects of Teniers's life or style, but none has been entirely satisfactory.[3] Some are incomplete; others contain errors gleaned from earlier sources. None has dealt with the artist's stylistic evolution from his early works to the works of the mature Teniers.

This study seeks to present a more complete biography of Teniers along with a detailed analysis of his style in various periods of his career. The book discusses the artists who influenced Teniers and, in turn, those he influenced. It also contains material about the painters with whom Teniers collaborated. Finally, consideration is given to Teniers as a graphic artist and to his impact on the graphic arts. The study provides a basis for Teniers's connoisseurship that will facilitate the difficult problem of dating the large number of his undated works. It may also shed some light on the problems of sorting out the many followers and imitators of Teniers.

It has not been my intention to prepare a catalogue raisonné. I am aware that this may prove disappointing to some who seek an analysis of several thousand boring genres and landscapes. I attempt here to establish new, accurate criteria for the recognition of Teniers's paintings and for the artist's stylistic evolution. It does not seem right to place Teniers in the mold of an artist such as Van Dyck, always the prodigy. There is a definite evolutionary sequence in Teniers's paintings and this sequence is my primary consideration. I could see no reason to bore the reader with endlessly repetitive peasant genres.

Jane P. Davidson

Acknowledgments

I am indebted to a great many people for their assistance in the preparation of this study. First of all, I must thank Erik Larsen, who first suggested that I study Teniers and who has continued to be interested in my research over the years.

I would also like to thank the staffs of several research institutions for their help with details of Teniers's life and with documentation of various paintings. The staffs of the Archives générales du royaume, Brussels, and the Archives de la Ville de Bruxelles come to mind, as does the staff of the Stadsarchief, Antwerp. The staff of the Rijksbureau voor Kunsthistorische Documentatie, the Institut royal du patrimoine artistique, and the Zentral Institut für Kunstgeschichte were also most helpful. I especially thank Dr. Ulla Krempel of the Direktion der Bayerischen Staatsgemäldesammlungen, who on several occasions shared her expertise and helped me obtain information on paintings in the Alte Pinakothek and the Schleissheim collections.

Many museum staff members have been of great help to me over the years, but I am indebted in a special way to Jacques Foucart of the Louvre, who was most kind to me.

My husband provided me with a never-failing sounding board and with much insight into the artistic mind. He also served as my research technician in unlocking the secrets of the pigments Teniers used in his famous grey glazes. Finally, I cannot fail to offer special thanks to those generous individuals who made possible the printing of the plates for this book and thus its publication.

J. P. D.

Introduction

David Teniers the Younger, painter of the commonplace and drollery, was considered by his contemporaries an artist of sufficient stature to warrant his inclusion in several seventeenth-century lexica. His life was first recorded by De Bie,[1] and accounts of his activities also appeared in Roger de Piles's *Abrégé de la vie des peintres*[2] and in von Sandrart's *Teutsche Academie*.[3] None of these biographers provided much information on Teniers's style.

Five biographical collections of the eighteenth century contain accounts of the life of Teniers the Younger. They are more extensive than their seventeenth-century predecessors, but they also contain erroneous statements (which were later assimilated by nineteenth-century scholars). The eighteenth-century biographies are all quite similar. The earliest, and the best, is found in Houbraken's *Groote Schouburgh*.[4] This volume was followed by Campo-Weyermann's lexicon, published in 1729, which is noteworthy only for its mention of the relationship between Teniers and Jan Brueghel I.

Teniers next appears in Descamps's *Vie des peintres flamands et hollandais*.[5] Descamps was responsible for a number of mistakes concerning the life of Teniers, but his account is interesting for its list of the artist's paintings in eighteenth-century French collections. It was Descamps who first stated that Teniers derived his characteristic "silvery tonalities" from the example of Rubens's underpainting. This incorrect idea has persisted, appearing in Max Doerner's *The Materials of the Artist and Their Use in Painting* as recently as 1949.[6]

Teniers's life was included in Dezailler d'Argenville's *Abrégé de la vie des plus fameux peintres* in 1762[7] and Mariette's *Abecedario*.[8] These two works probably provided the basis for the controversy surrounding the date of Teniers's death. Dezailler d'Argenville wrote that Teniers died in 1694; however, Mariette was the only eighteenth-century biographer to correctly identify the date of the artist's death as 1690. The problem has apparently

1

not yet been laid to rest, for one still occasionally finds the year of Teniers's death given as 1694.

It is possible to reconstruct the Teniers family lineage in fairly great detail. The Teniers family apparently may be traced to Jehan de Taisnière à Caumes, who resided in or around Mons. An entry in the charter of the Chapter of St. Waldrue of Mons, dated October 28, 1340, mentions this man.[9] The Taisnières of Caumes probably migrated to Brugelette.[10] The family is first mentioned as residents there in a document deposited in the municipal records of Ath in 1460.[11] It is the Ath branch of the Taisnières who were the apparent ancestors of David Teniers the Younger.

David Teniers's lineage can be traced with certainty to Thomas Taisnière and Catherine de l'Issue, who resided in Ath during the first half of the sixteenth century. The third son of Thomas Taisnière, a certain Joachim Taisnière, became the father of Julian Teniers of Antwerp, and thus the grandfather of David Teniers the Younger.[12]

The lives of Julian Joachimzoon Teniers and his son David Teniers the Elder are well documented and need not be discussed here.[13] With the establishment of David the Elder as a prominent Antwerp artist we come to the first years of the life of David the Younger.

We will see that even in the beginning of his artistic career, David the Younger's style was something quite different from that of his high-baroque contemporaries, Rubens and Van Dyck. As we analyze Teniers's style we will find that it, too, was baroque, but consisted of quiet nuances rather than theatrical flamboyance. David the Younger's *"quiet baroque"* was actually more characteristic of most art in seventeenth-century Flanders than were the styles of Rubens and Van Dyck. His style has much in common with that of the high-baroque masters—his paintings are undeniably baroque, yet they are subtle. His is a record of the century told in quiet, precise terms. The pictures tell of the lives and beliefs of the Flemings, but they never overwhelm the viewer. The style is understandable, but it does not shout out its messages. It is the "quiet baroque."

1 Teniers's Life and Style: 1610-1650

TENIERS'S LIFE

Nothing is known of Teniers's childhood or early education. In view of his later services as a courtier and business agent to Archduke Leopold Wilhelm it may be safely presumed that he did receive some formal education. Obviously he must have seen the works of the great masters with whom his father associated and collaborated. This background, along with the training he received from his father, formed the basis for the development of Teniers's personal style. David the Younger's training as a painter seems to have come entirely from his father, but we know that he assimilated other ideas on his own.

The name of David Teniers the Younger first emerges from the obscurity of his childhood in a document mentioned by van den Branden. This was a deposition, dated January 12, 1628, given by Teniers's father and witnessed by David the Younger.[1] In the following year, David the Elder was imprisoned in the Steen, the Antwerp city prison, for raising an illegal second mortgage and for nonpayment of debts.[2] On July 12, 1629, David the Younger petitioned for power of attorney for his father in order to conduct transactions that would enable the elder Teniers to pay off his creditors. The archives are silent again on the activities of David the Younger until 1632 when his name was entered in the *Liggeren* of the Antwerp Guild of St. Luke.[3]

Van den Branden believed that David Teniers the Elder had been in Paris in 1635, but it is possible that it was actually David the Younger who made the journey. The Antwerp *Paspoortenboek* (passport record book) for the years 1632 to 1648 records a passport issued to a David Teniers in 1635.[4] David Teniers is also mentioned in the "List van kunstenaars, handelaars, en boekdrukkers" (list of fine artists, art dealers, and book dealers) who appeared before the Brabantsche Lotkamer on January 13, 1635.[5] These documents are probably the sources of van den Branden's statement, although the mere presence of the name "David Teniers" does not substantiate which of the two artists had obtained the passport and had appeared before the Lotkamer. Both Teniers the Elder and Teniers the Younger were referred to as David Teniers. For example, David the Younger is called both "David Teniers" and "David Teniers the Younger" in his marriage contract. That David the Younger may have gone to Paris in 1635 is substantiated by the fact that we know he was in Dover during this year. A contract between him and the art dealer Chrisostome van Immerseel, dated "in Douvers den 29 Decembre 1635," provides proof of this.[6] That it was Teniers the Younger with whom van Immerseel dealt is made clear by a letter that van Immerseel wrote to his agent in Antwerp on March 26, 1636. This letter concerned payments to be made to Teniers.

Aen een Joncman genaempt Sr. David Tesniers woonende in Ul streate, bestedde aen, in Douveren, voor my to doen maecken ende schilderen twelfve copere plaeten griecquen ofte wat grooter, voor hondert gulden . . . eene Drollerye naer Brauwer.[7]

To a bachelor named David Teniers who lives in your city, paid to (him) in Dover, to make and paint for me twelve copper panels, griequen never larger, for one hundred guilders . . . a drollery after Brouwer.

Van Immerseel's reference to *Joncman* (bachelor) David Teniers clarifies which David Teniers had made the contract. It is apparent that David the Younger was a well established and successful artist by 1636. Not only were his works sold abroad by prominent dealers, but he was considered an artist of enough importance to receive a commission from Rubens to furnish a painting for the Torre de la Parada, the hunting lodge of the king of Spain. The work, a scene of dancing peasants, has been destroyed and is known only from an entry in the catalog of the Torre de la Parada paintings. One may assume that it was a typical peasant kermis.[8]

Rubens was a personal friend of Teniers. He had been one of the guardians of Anna Brueghel, daughter of Jan Brueghel I, whom Teniers married in 1637. Anna herself must have known David the Younger all her life, as her father collaborated with David Teniers the Elder on occasion. The couple signed their marriage contract on July 4, 1637, with Rubens as a witness. Their marriage took place in the St. Jacobskerk on July 22.[9]

During the 1630s David the Younger continued to be successful in obtaining commissions at home and from abroad. Contracts with van Immerseel, dated 1637 and 1638, indicate that he ordered twenty-six paintings from Teniers during these two years. Since van Immerseel was operating his art business from Seville at this time, these paintings must have been destined for foreign markets.[10]

The joint testament of David Teniers the Younger and Anna Brueghel, prepared in 1638, provides some indication as to Teniers's financial status at that time. In this testament David the Younger left the sum of one hundred guldens each to his three brothers and to his sister Anne.[11] The drafting of this testament may have been occasioned by Anna Brueghel's pregnancy. The first of the couple's seven children was born in July 1638. The boy was baptized David Teniers III on July 10, in the St. Jacobskerk. His godparents were David Teniers the Elder and Helene Fourment, Rubens's wife.[12]

In 1639 David the Younger leased the house called St. Hendrick in the Everdrijstraat for a period of four years. Here he lived with his growing family until 1642.[13]

The Antwerp passport records indicate that David Teniers, "schilder en kunsthandlaar" (painter and art dealer), obtained passports in 1640 and again in 1641.[14] If these were granted to David the Younger, they would prove that he was dealing in art himself by at least this time. The whole Teniers family seems to have been in the art business during these years. Passports were also granted in 1640 to Julian II and Theodore Teniers, David's brothers. Presumably these three travelled together in order to conduct transactions. They may have also worked in conjunction with their father, as David the Elder is known to have dealt in art as well.

Relations between the Teniers and Brueghel families seem to have always been close and amicable. David the Younger became the acting guardian of the estate of Ambroise and Claire-Eugénie Brueghel (Anna's brother and sister) in 1641,[15] and Ambroise and Claire-Eugénie later served as godparents to two of David the Younger's children.[16]

David the Younger's talents began to reach their fullest expression during the 1640s. In this decade he received commissions from a number of important clients. In 1643 he painted two works that are considered among his masterpieces. These are the *Fat Kitchen,* Plate 7, and *The Parade of the St. Joris Shooting Guild of Antwerp* (Leningrad, The Hermitage Museum). By the end of this decade David the Younger would be one of the leading artists of the Southern Netherlands, much in demand by several royal patrons as well as by the general public. He was also accepted by his fellow artists as a master of distinction. While David the Younger never had a large number of students, those he did take worked under his tutelage in the 1640s and are discussed in Chapter 4.

David the Younger served as dean of the Guild of St. Luke in 1645 and 1646 and was active as a member of the Violieren Chamber of Rhetoric, an adjunct of the Guild, at this time.[17] By 1647 David the Younger was well known throughout the Southern Netherlands. Antoon Triest, the distinguished bishop of Ghent, ordered a number of paintings from him between the years 1645 and 1647. The fact that Teniers named his second son after the bishop, who was godfather by proxy, indicates that Triest must have been satisfied with the paintings he had purchased.

Late in 1647 Teniers embarked on the most important phase of his artistic career. Two documents dated December 16 and December 18, 1647, respectively, prove that he was now in the service of Archduke Leopold

Wilhelm. These documents do not clearly specify all of Teniers's activities for the archduke, but it is certain that he now furnished his own paintings to the Brussels court. Since Leopold Wilhelm had only governed the Southern Netherlands since April 1647, Teniers must have been in his employ almost from the beginning of the archduke's governorship. The two documents of 1647 are receipts of payments made to Teniers by Leopold Wilhelm's treasurer, Don Julian Dellano Velasco. The first is fairly brief, but it does indicate that David the Younger was working part-time in Brussels: "Al pintor llamado Teniers, qui travazo en palacio en las piezas de marmo, he pagado aqui los 300 patacones."[18] The second document discloses that Teniers was still residing in Antwerp at this time as it specifically mentions Teniers as a resident of Antwerp.[19]

There is a strong possibility that Teniers may have come to the archduke's attention through an introduction by Bishop Triest. Triest, who was quite pleased with David the Younger's paintings, was a well-known figure in Brussels society and a frequenter of the archducal court.[20] If Teniers was not brought to the archduke's attention by Triest or some other dignitary, he may have come forward himself to offer his services to the governor. David the Younger seems always to have been an opportunist where his career was concerned. He certainly would not have let pass the chance of obtaining important commissions for lack of boldness.[21]

Records in the Stadsarchief, Antwerp, indicate that David the Younger still lived in Antwerp in 1649 where he appeard as a witness in a civil suit in November of that year.[22] While he was undoubtedly also in the employ of the archduke, Teniers continued to pursue his own career as an independent artist during the last years of the decade. It was during 1649 that he executed an important commission for William of Orange, the stadtholder of the United Netherlands. The painting, entitled *Village Festival*, may possibly be the one that is now in the royal collection at Buckingham Palace. A preparatory drawing exists for this or some very similar work. The drawing bears Teniers's signature and the date 1649, as well as the following inscription.

> Monsieur Teniers zal gelieven to schilderen voor sijne hoocheyt Minne herre den Prin(ce) van orange deeze ondergeteyskende boer karmis.[23]

> M. Teniers shall promise to paint for his majesty the Prince of Orange this peasant festival drawn below.

David the Younger's activities during this decade of his career indicate that his growth in popularity was as steady as his artistic development will shortly be seen to have been. It has been observed that David the Younger gained in reputation at a fairly steady rate after his entry into the Guild of St. Luke. Such an expanding career, one which would soon include international royal patrons, cannot be explained unless the artist had not improved his style with the passing years. The early works of David the Younger were reasonably good, but were not the paintings of a great master. They by no means compare with Teniers's contemporaries in the 1630s, Rubens and Van Dyck. Even David the Younger's Brouwer-style paintings from this period were not sufficiently good to bring him the international royal acclaim he was shortly to enjoy. We cannot possibly ascribe David the Younger's increasing popularity to the influential position held by his father. David the Elder was by no means an important master himself.[24]

We are forced to conclude, even before examining his paintings, that David the Younger must have improved considerably in the period 1632 to 1646. When we do examine the paintings from this period we find that this growth did indeed take place. In fact, David the Younger's first decade may be characterized by two distinct periods. These are an early period and a transitional period, which is here called his early-mature period.

TENIERS'S EARLY STYLE

As one might expect, the early paintings of David the Younger display a blend of influences, some of which extend into his mature period, and several stages of stylistic development, to be discussed in detail later. The artist's brushstroke is always fairly easy to recognize and appears in even his earliest works. This fact serves to facilitate the task of identifying early paintings. Some of these are rather crudely executed and dark in color, and only Teniers's individual brushstroke makes identification of these works possible. They would otherwise remain consigned to that already troublesome group of paintings attributed to the David Teniers, father and son.

Paintings in the early style (to about 1640) show an ever increasing degree of technical skill and compositional sophistication. They reveal the influences of several masters who contributed to the development of Teniers's style and iconography. These artists greatly influenced Teniers's paintings, which may be seen even in mature-period works. They are David Teniers the Elder, Adriaen Brouwer, Pieter Brueghel I, Pieter Brueghel II, Jan Brueghel I, and Frans Francken II. Of these the most significant contributors to Teniers's style were Brouwer and the Brueghels. While Brouwer's influence was important, it has been overestimated. The time-honored scholarly practice of describing Teniers as a follower of Brouwer has tended to cause historians to overlook the great importance of the Brueghelian tradition in David the Younger's art. This influence was not merely because of his interest in peasant genres—Teniers's relationship to the Brueghels goes much deeper than this and was far more significant and lasting than his interest in Brouwer's style. Teniers's study of Brouwer lasted only for a period of about ten years. While Brouwer's influence was important in the development of Teniers's style, it is shown below that it is best to consider Teniers as a member of the Brueghelian circle.

Influence of David the Elder. The first discernable influence in the early style of David the Younger is that of his father and only teacher, David the Elder. This is indicated by the young Teniers's entry in 1632-1633 into the Antwerp Guild of St. Luke as a *wynmeester* (an apprenticeship in the guild offered only to sons of masters). Further, there exists no record of David the Younger ever having studied with masters other than his father.[25]

The art of the youthful Teniers already contains the seeds of his mature style but may be described best as a style marked by conflicts between the late mannerism of David the Elder and the evolving baroque style of the first quarter of the seventeenth century in Flanders. David the Younger worked in collaboration with his father on at least one series of paintings, executed about 1628 to 1630. (See Appendix for a further discussion of the dating of this series.) These are twelve panels that comprise a series of episodes from Tasso's epic *Gerusalemme Liberata.* The paintings are executed primarily in the style of David the Elder, although eleven of them contain the already identifiable brushstroke and steadier draftsmanhip of David the Younger. The attribution of these paintings has had a varied history. Today, the Prado catalogs them under the works of David Teniers the Elder. They are also seen credited to David the Younger in older literature. However, this study is the first known to recognize the paintings for what they actually are, collaborations between father and son.

In the Tasso paintings, David the Younger's handling of paint still appears somewhat hesitant, but nonetheless his abilities were beginning to surpass those of David the Elder even at this early date. The series was executed on copper panels measuring twenty-seven by thirty-nine centimeters. The little paintings have been cleaned and are in generally good condition with the exception of some small areas from which paint has fallen away. These areas reveal that David the Elder used very thin preparations for his paintings, a practice adopted by his son. David the Younger's contributions are mainly found in the background landscapes, skies, and some details of drapery and still life. His role was clearly that of an assistant. That the paintings were partially the work of David the Younger is further substantiated by the youthful appearance of Teniers, who served as the model for Rinaldo—depicted as a man in his late teens or early twenties.

While Teniers the Younger was still serving as an assistant at this point he had already begun to modify the compositional techniques of David the Elder towards a more baroque pictorial style. The compositions remain similar to those used by David the Elder, but they are not typical of his usual mannerist principles of organization. An examination of the background landscapes of the series reveals a subtle conflict between David the Elder's compositional devices and those being developed by David the Younger. The combination of styles, although noticeable, is reasonably agreeable. However, the compositions do tend to disintegrate and are much less satisfactory upon close scrutiny.

Three scenes from the Tasso series will serve to demonstrate the conflict of styles found in these panels. The landscape of *Charles and Ubald Tempted by Nymphs*, Plate 8, is composed of trees that curtain off the horizon and force the observer's attention to the foreground plane. The composition is opened up slightly at the right. A very weak diagonal, created by the break in the trees in the center, contributes only in a small degree to the feeling of recession.

A similar forest backdrop may be found in a painting of *Minerva Visiting the Muses* (private collection, Switzerland) by David the Elder.[26] In this work the forest so completely cuts off the background that it destroys any possible sense of recession. There is a small opening at the right that reveals a little of the horizon, but with typical mannerist ambiguity this portion of the composition seems almost unrelated to the rest of the painting.

The background in the *Dream of Oradine*, Plate 9, has been treated in a manner similar to that of *Charles and Ubald Tempted by Nymphs,* but the composition is now opened up to a greater degree by two rather pronounced diagonals at the right and center of the scene. These direct the eye to a low horizon. The left foreground is entirely filled in by trees, foliage, and the figure of the sleeping Oradine. These elements are arranged along another weak diagonal that increases the sense of recession. The figures of Oradine and the demon Clorinda are placed prominently in the foreground, but they are better integrated into their surroundings than are the figures of Charles and Ubald.

The treatment of the background in the *Dream of Oradine* seems related to some other compositions by David the Elder, such as *The Meeting of Jacob and Laban* (Antwerp, Maagdenhuis), but in the *Dream of Oradine* the composition is marked by a more sophisticated handling of spatial components, which creates a coherent scene. The visual distractions that exist in *The Meeting of Jacob and Laban* no longer are found in the *Dream of Oradine.* This increased degree of organization probably indicates the presence of the hand of David the Younger. This is further indicated by an analysis of the brushstrokes, which reveals his hand in the background and probably in the figure of Clorinda.

In the panel depicting *Charles and Ubald Searching for Rinaldo*, Plate 10, the background is very similar to those found in the mature works of David the Younger. The right half of the scene is almost completely filled by a cave and forest placed on a strongly receding diagonal. This diagonal is reinforced by the river that flows past the mouth of the cave. The horizon now is quite low. The composition has become more aesthetically pleasing and is not unlike landscape backgrounds used by many Flemish masters in the 1620s. As in the *Dream of Oradine*, the figures integrate well with the composition. The background elements no longer form a "stage," for they have become an important part of the whole scene.

The compositional diversity in this series may indicate that Teniers the Elder was coming under the influence of his son, who was obviously aware of the newer trends of Flemish baroque landscapes. In fact Teniers the Younger may have designed some of the compositions himself. While the panels are generally lacking in quality, they do provide an interesting document in the development of the early style of David the Younger. The artist's love for delicately painted areas of still life and drapery, as well as his precisely drawn features of anatomy, were taking form in these panels. These paintings have been attributed to both David Teniers, father and son, as stated earlier. They do bear the signature of David the Elder, but they contain far too many compositional and stylistic discrepancies to have been produced exclusively by either artist. They are a definite case of collaboration, a mannerist-baroque hybrid.

While David the Younger was never a mannerist, his paintings continued to show the lingering influence of his father. This influence extends even into David the Younger's mature period. He adopted his father's landscape-with-figure compositions, giving them a more baroque, pictorial quality but still retaining the use of important foreground elements, receding diagonals, background *staffage,* and cloud-filled skies found in the paintings of David the Elder. Teniers the Younger's scenes always appear better organized and yet more loosely structured. Important figures are never placed before the landscape but are integrated into the composition. In some paintings the landscape becomes almost more important than the figures. This is quite common in Teniers's numerous landscapes, which frequently contain few figures or architectural elements. The diagonal is always a prominent organizational feature and is often reinforced by landscape features in the foreground. Such is the case in the beautiful *St. Anthony in a Landscape,* Plate 1, a painting from his mature period.

Two of David the Younger's other paintings from the 1660s, the mature period, demonstrate the continuing influence of David the Elder's compositions. In this decade David the Younger painted a series of fifteen small panels that depict the *Fifteen Mysteries of the Rosary* (Munich, Alte Pinakothek).[27] Each is signed and while they are relatively unknown, they are certainly the work of David the Younger. The artist maintained a fairly high level of technical quality throughout the series and the scenes function well together as a unit. This group is unique since it is apparently the only series of New Testament subjects David the Younger ever executed. The panels depicting *Christ on the Mount of Olives* and *The Nativity* were based on paintings by David the Elder.

David the Elder painted a *Christ on the Mount of Olives* for the Church of

St. Paul in Antwerp. The painting, in situ, seems in poor condition, but enough detail remains to prove that this work was the basis for the painting by David the Younger in the *Mysteries of the Rosary* series. The scene is rendered in the mannerist style of David the Elder and reveals his dependence on the lighting techniques of Elsheimer.[28] The composition is not well coordinated and is filled with the mannerists' tendencies towards structural ambiguities and tensions.

In contrast, the painting of *Christ on the Mount of Olives* (Plate 11) by David the Younger is a fully developed, baroque composition containing much better integrated forms, more dramatic lighting, and a better balanced composition. Yet its composition remains close enough to that of the painting by David the Elder to indicate that it was this work that David the Younger had in mind when he painted the series. While *Christ on the Mount of Olives* was based on one painting by David the Elder, *The Nativity*, Plate 12, was probably based on more than one version by Teniers the Elder.[29] The major source of influence seems to be a painting of *The Shepherds's Visit* (New York, Mary van Berg collection). In this work David the Elder again revealed his typical mannerist technique of forcing the action into the foreground plane. Strong contrasts of light and shade are once more employed. The composition is quite linear and flat and there is no use of the diagonal. The definite mannerist style of this work indicates that it must have been painted before Teniers the Elder came under the influence of his son, probably before 1640.

The question of mutual influence between father and son cannot be overlooked. David the Elder did not die until 1649 and it seems clear that he began to copy paintings by his son during the last decades of his life. There is the case, for example, of the painting by David the Elder, *Interior of an Inn* (London, Vanderkerkar Gallery, 1969), which is an exact copy of David the Younger's *Imperial Kitchen* (Leningrad, The Hermitage), dated 1646. Further, Teniers the Younger himself used certain stereotyped figures that he derived from Teniers the Elder. Thus his females in *The Witch* (Plate 4) and *The Prodigal Son with the Prostitutes* (Plate 22) are derived from the stereotyped females of David the Elder. This problem of authorship of individual paintings cannot merely be dismissed by assigning seemingly inferior looking paintings to David the Elder. To do this is to deny the concept of an early period in the style of David the Younger. This period quite clearly exists.

A more carefully detailed study of the style and chronology of David the Elder's paintings is needed at this point. Such a study would be much easier than has been supposed since there is a distinct difference between the brushstrokes of the two artists.

Influence of Adriaen Brouwer. Adriaen Brouwer exerted the most obvious and profound influence on the style of David the Younger of all the masters with whom he had contact. The degree of this influence exceeds even that of David Teniers the Elder. David the Younger not only adopted Brouwer's color schemes and general compositions, he also appropriated whole figures from Brouwer's paintings making virtually no changes to disguise their origin. He came so close to Brouwer's style that it is almost impossible to distinguish certain of his paintings from Brouwer's without a careful examination of the brushstrokes.

David the Younger made drawings after paintings by Brouwer. A drawing of *Card Players*, Plate 13, contains the figure of an old innkeeper holding a tankard. This figure is placed in a pose very similar to that of the central figure in Brouwer's *Innkeeper* (Munich, Alte Pinakothek). The Munich *Innkeeper* may not necessarily have been the direct source for this drawing since the pose of a man slumped over in a chair holding a tankard at his side is seen frequently in Brouwer's paintings. It does, however, point out Teniers's close observation of Brouwer's work.

While David the Younger copied the paintings of other Flemish masters, he never took whole figures from the paintings of any artist except Brouwer. It is as though he were studying Brouwer's style as he copied the paintings. Certain Teniers paintings are very close copies of Brouwer's works. For example, David the Younger's *Le Roi Boit*, Plate 14, is greatly dependent on Brouwer's famous *The Smoker* (New York, Metropolitan Museum of Art). The arrangement of figures in both paintings is practically the same; David the Younger copied the central smoking figure directly from the Brouwer painting. A similar smoking *boer* (peasant) is found in another painting from slightly later in Teniers's early period entitled *The Smoker*, Plate 15. This was probably painted about 1643 and is most likely a portrait of one of the artist's brothers: either Jean Baptiste, who would have been thirty at this time; or possibly Julien III, who was twenty-seven in 1643. Whoever this person is, he is certainly one of the Teniers family and bears a distinct resemblance to David the Younger despite the fact that he has been made to appear somewhat crude of features as befits the pose of a *boer*. This deliberate roughening of features is quite common in Teniers's genre paintings in which he used members of his family as models. One sees Anna Brueghel—the artist's wife—for example, appearing among the witches in many Teniers's paintings of sabbats. She is always clearly identifiable, but her features and her demeanor are coarsened in keeping with the evil creature she is made to represent.

In his paintings of an *Interior of an Inn* (Cleveland Museum of Art), David the Younger again displayed his close affiliation with Brouwer's figure types. The seated peasant who prepares to light his pipe recalls similar smoking peasants found in many Brouwer paintings. The peasants in Brouwer's *Smoking Boers* (Staatliche Kunstsammlung, Kassel) are good examples of such types. Teniers also painted several scenes of drinking figures whose poses were probably derived from Brouwer. The drinker in

Teniers's *Interior of a Tavern* (London, Herner Wengraf Gallery, 1974) is placed in a pose that is quite like that of the sleeping landlord in the Munich *Innkeeper*. [30]

Paintings by David the Younger also include other Brouwer-inspired characters, such as pancake women, village surgeons, quack doctors, and the like. The *Interior of an Inn* (London, National Gallery) contains the figure of a woman preparing pancakes that is based on Brouwer's *Pancake Woman* (Philadelphia, Museum of Art, John G. Johnson collection).

The 1652 inventory of Rubens's estate listed a painting of *The Temptations of St. Anthony* by Brouwer. Since this painting has disappeared, there is no way of determining whether it had any influence on the numerous versions of the theme by Teniers. However, an early painting of the *Temptations of St. Anthony* (Paris, Ader and Picard, 1969), dated 1637, contains demon peasants who are rather similar to the peasants of Brouwer. The boer who has conjured up several denizens of the underworld in Tenier's *Evocation* (Bordeaux Musée des Beaux-Arts) also recalls Brouwer's peasant types. It may be that Teniers's use of crude peasants in this context comes from Brouwer. This supposition is reinforced by the fact that Teniers was so well acquainted with the Brouwer peasant.

David the Younger may have become interested in Brouwer's paintings as early as 1631, when Brouwer arrived in Antwerp. Since Brouwer seems to have remained in the city for most of the time between 1631 and his death in 1638,[31] Teniers would have had ample opportunity to have become thoroughly acquainted with Brouwer's technique. Perhaps they first met when David the Younger entered the Guild of St. Luke in 1632, or perhaps Rubens may have introduced them. Considering the close association of Antwerp artists, an occasion for their meeting would have posed no difficulty.

It does seem that the two painters must have had a fairly close association from 1635 to 1638. Teniers's paintings in his Brouwer style seem to be most closely related to Brouwer paintings from this period. Gerard Knuttel has written that during the last years of his life Brouwer developed a palette based on subtle blends of browns with little use of local color.[32] To this must be added the greyish overtones also found in later Brouwer works. It was this color scheme that attracted David the Younger. He employed Brouwer's brown and grey tonalities but tended to include more descriptive color in his paintings than did Brouwer. Generally Teniers achieved the relief in tonality by the use of stronger, clearer reds and a purer shade of blue than used by Brouwer. The greys in both Brouwer's and Teniers's paintings were derived from overpainting with glazes of a combination of white, raw umber, and azurite blue.

Descamps's belief that Teniers obtained his grey or silvery tones from underpainting is without basis in fact. An examination of paintings by both Brouwer and Teniers that contain these greys reveals that the tones were laid in over the rest of the paint. Moreover, this type of tonality cannot be reproduced by underpainting. I had experiments conducted using such glazes in situations of underpainting and overpainting.[33] The grey tonalities were achieved only when the glazes were applied over the painting's surface.

Teniers must have mixed his grey glazes using two parts azurite blue to one part each of white and raw umber. The experiments proved this to be the most satisfactory combination of pigments. Other combinations resulted in greenish or black shades. The grey thus achieved cannot be derived from mixing black and white. Furthermore, in order to arrive at Teniers's and Brouwer's grey tones, one must lay the grey glaze in over an umber background. An examination of the actual paintings shows that this is precisely what the two artists did themselves.

Teniers's grey tones were most certainly derived from Brouwer. They appear in late Brouwer paintings, such as the *Bitter Drink* and the *Foot Operation* (Frankfurt, Staedelsches Kunstinstitut).[34] David the Younger used this technique not only in his Brouwer-style paintings but also in works executed in his mature style and palette. He reduced the intensity in his greys in his mature period, however, as can be seen in the grey tones of *The Alchemist* (Plate 26), for example. This painting is in Teniers's mature style but still contains passages of lighter grey obtained through the use of glazes. Despite his concession to his lighter palette, the grey tones are still distinctive enough to play an important role in the color scheme of the painting.

Teniers probably began to experiment with grey tone about 1635, at approximately the same time Brouwer began to use the technique with greater frequency in his own paintings. A *Still Life*, Plate 2, dated 1635, already contains greys obtained through the use of overpainting. This Teniers painting is carefully composed, the draftsmanship is excellent, and considerable attention is paid to detail. Yet this work may have been only a study in Brouwer's color schemes executed for Teniers's own purposes as his still lifes are extremely rare; they are certainly not the type of paintings he sold.

The panel depicts a group of books, maps, and a globe piled on a table. The table top and the objects on it nearly fill the composition. The table is placed in the corner of a room, and it is on the walls that Teniers used his grey glazes. A limited amount of grey was also used on some of the books and the globe. There is almost no local color in the painting, it being essentially a study in brown and grey tonal harmonies.

Some paintings that Teniers executed on copper also display a distinctive light silvery cast. The *Fat Kitchen* (Plate 7) is one of the best examples of this type. The situation with respect to copper panels is sometimes unique. At times the silvery grey tones are not derived from glazes, but rather result from chemical changes in the pigments brought about by the oxidation of the copper plate. That this is the case in the *Fat Kitchen* may be demonstrated by the fact that whole sections of the painting have turned grey. The background contains grey passages, but the same greys are also in evidence in areas of local color, such as the clothing of the central figures and the still life elements. Grey tones produced by oxidation conform to neither the color scheme of a painting nor its brushstrokes and therefore are easily identified. Teniers continued to paint Brouwer-style paintings at least until the end of his early-mature period, about 1644, when he painted the *Boers's Carouse* (London, Wallace Collection). In this painting, the peasants are more Teniersian, but the stamp of Brouwer is still strongly felt.

To speak of Teniers as a follower of Brouwer is not actually appropriate because his study of Brouwer was essentially a technical exercise. The fascination he had with Brouwer lasted only about ten years, during Teniers's formative period. He was *studying* Brouwer. However, Teniers went beyond Brouwer to evolve his own personal style. His interest in Brouwer seems to have been only one element in his development as an artist. Indeed, the mature style of Teniers has its seeds in his earliest works from the 1630s and contains many other elements besides those he derived from his technical study of Brouwer. Teniers's Brouwer period is one of unusually close dependence upon another master; a strong reflection of eclecticism in an artist who was to be eclectic always.

Influence of the Brueghels. A long-overlooked—but obvious and important—source of influence in Teniers's art is that of the Brueghel tradition. In fact, Teniers seems to fit better among the followers of the Brueghels than he does among those of Brouwer. The subject matter and iconography most evident in David the Younger's paintings (with the exception of his personal iconography) are those derived from the Brueghels. Generally, this influence comes from paintings by the Pieter Brueghels I and II, but Teniers was also influenced to a limited degree by Jan Brueghel I. While most of this influence comes directly from the Brueghels themselves, there are also a few Brueghelian themes that were probably transmitted through works by Frans Francken II. His contribution to Teniers's paintings is discussed shortly.

Because of his lifelong association with the Brueghel family, it might seem natural to look for and to find Brueghelian iconography and themes in Teniers's paintings. Yet this source of influence has been largely ignored. David the Younger's paintings of witches, his *Temptations of St. Anthony*, and other scenes that depict aspects of the underworld have always been noted for their similarities to the paintings and engravings of the same themes by Pieter Brueghel I. Similarly, much has been written about the obvious relationships between the peasant genres of Teniers and those of the Brueghels. With respect to peasant scenes, it is quite clear that Teniers was deeply influenced by the Brueghels. His peasant kermises are not in the least different from those of the two Pieters, nor are his other genres really different from those that the Brueghels created.

By virtue of the vast numbers of Teniers's peasant genres, all so similar to the genres of the Brueghels, one might cease discussion of Teniers as a Brueghelian at this point alone. Clearly genres were his most popular productions, but the relationship between his paintings and their iconography and those of the Brueghels go much deeper than this. Teniers was not merely another genrist in the Brueghel *sillage* (circle of followers). His paintings were closely aligned with the full extent of Brueghelian iconography, which extended to representations of religious and mythological themes, alchemy, and the occult. In all these categories we find paintings by Teniers that reveal his heritage from the Brueghels.

The strong resemblance between David the Younger's grotesques and those of Pieter Brueghel I would not in itself constitute a forceful argument for a close relationship between the iconography as used by both men. However, a painting of *The Temptations of St. Anthony,* Plate 16, proves that Teniers made a detailed study of Pieter I's iconography. This painting is most unusual in the Teniers repertoire of St. Anthonies as it is the only one in which David the Younger depicted St. Anthony being accosted by allegorical figures of the "Seven Deadly Sins." The painting shows St. Anthony at prayer in the usual grotto with a typical collection of music-making demons and other grotesque figures. The demon prostitute frequently found in *Temptations of St. Anthony* is present, but the iconography of this painting is based almost entirely upon the series of engravings, *The Seven Deadly Sins* (located in various European museums), executed by Pieter I about 1557.

In Teniers's *Temptations of St. Anthony,* his prostitute always represents the temptation to lust, but in this version she is presented to St. Anthony not by a witch—as is the usual case, but rather by a well-dressed youth, carrying a peacock, who represents the sin of pride. The pair is escorted by Cupid—identifiable by his bow—who further signifies the sin of lust. Pieter I's engraving of *Pride* contains a peacock, while prostitute witches are found in his engraving of *Lust.*

The other "deadly sins" surround the personifications of lust and pride. Avarice is found at the extreme right of the composition. This sin is represented by an old woman, seated among money bags, who is weighing coins on a scale. Money and scales are traditional attributes of avarice and were used by Pieter I in his engraving of the same name. Opposite Avarice are Anger and Envy. Anger is a woman brandishing a large knife and riding a lion. The lion did not appear in the Brueghel engraving of *Anger,* but the print is filled with the symbolism of knives, scissors, and other sharp instruments, which signify the violence associated with the sin. Envy is a man shown in the act of eating his heart. In Pieter I's engraving of *Envy* the allegorical figure representing the sin also eats her heart. Teniers placed Sloth and Gluttony at the entrance to the grotto. Sloth is represented by a tired woman who rides a donkey. She leans on one elbow and seems about to fall asleep. This figure is derived from the sad sleeping woman reclining on a donkey in the Brueghel engraving of *Sloth*.

Gluttony is the most interesting of Teniers's allegories. It is not based on Brueghelian iconography but is personified by Hans Worst, the buffoon who appears in contemporary Flemish literature. Hans Worst, or Gluttony, wears his traditional garland of sausages and carries a wine glass in one hand and a jug in the other. Hans Worst was frequently associated with gluttony and overindulgence. He is found, for example, in Frans Hals's *Merry Company* (New York, Metropolitan Museum of Art) as one of the group of revelers. It was entirely appropriate that Teniers should use this character for this purpose.

The unusual treatment of this version of the *Temptations of St. Anthony* probably means that Teniers received a commission for the particular painting. The painting comes from his mature period and is the best example of Teniers's dependence on the iconography of Pieter Brueghel I.

Despite this careful study of Pieter I, most of Teniers's Brueghelian iconography comes from works by Pieter II. Besides creating his own *Seven Acts of Mercy* (Plate 3) after paintings of Pieter II, Teniers also copied Pieter's iconography in his one version of the *Flemish Proverbs* (formerly Belvoir Castle, Duke of Rutland). While David the Younger's *Flemish Proverbs* is closer to paintings by Pieter II, he must have known the *Flemish Proverbs* of Pieter I also. A painting on this theme by Pieter I was owned by the Antwerp collector Peter Stevens. Constantin Huygens II described this painting in Stevens's collection in 1676.[35]

Pieter II painted at least sixteen copies of the *Flemish Proverbs* himself.[36] The popularity of this theme in previous years may explain why Teniers did not paint it often. Perhaps there was no longer much demand for paintings of this particular topic. David the Younger's *Flemish Proverbs* was executed during his mature period and probably dates from the late 1640s. Teniers designed his *Proverbs* as a composition similar to that used by Pieter II, a village setting with a landscape background and typical Brueghelian "cutaway" houses, but he made several changes in the disposition of his figures. The composition of the picture is changed more, for example, than is Teniers's Louvre *Seven Acts of Mercy*, in which the figure groups are quite close to those of Pieter II. In David the Younger's *Flemish Proverbs* some figures were moved into entirely new positions within the composition. Some were deleted while others were added. These additions represent proverbs not found in the Brueghel paintings. For example, Teniers's painting contains two men seated on a roof playing fiddles. They may be a reference to the proverb of "the rich man's music," or *hij speelt op die hahe*. In the Brueghel versions of this proverb (including Pieter I's engraving), the man usually plays the jaw bone of an ass. Another proverb included by Teniers that does not come from the Brueghels is "the cat who watches a cheese." There are over forty proverbs illustrated in this painting and most of them are represented exactly as they were in the Brueghel paintings. For example, Teniers included those of the man who confesses to the Devil, the husband who drags a block of wood (a bad marriage), the pig wearing tongs, the monk who has thrown his habit over the fence, the gossips who spin thread and rumors, the blue mantle, the big fish eating the little fish, and the two dogs who fight over the same bone.[37] This painting is so closely dependent upon Brueghelian iconography that there can be no doubt as to the source of Teniers's theme.

David the Younger painted *Landscape with Christ and the Pilgrims to Emmaus*, Plate 17, in which he used the figures of Christ and the two pilgrims found in a painting by Pieter II of the same topic. The painting by Pieter II is in a private collection in Brussels.[38] A drawing of these figures in the Witt Library is probably a study by Teniers after Pieter II's painting. Teniers made some changes in the background of his version, but the central figures of Christ and the pilgrims are extremely close in dress, features, expressions, and gestures to those by Brueghel.

Teniers also derived some of his iconography and compositions from his father-in-law, Jan Brueghel I. Early paintings by Jan I of scenes of the underworld may have inspired some Teniers paintings of grotesque demons. There are also a few cases in which David the Younger has used Jan I's iconography for his own versions of the same subjects. For instance, David the Younger painted a *Juno in the Underworld* (Budapest, Josef Donath collection) whose composition is closely related to that used by Jan Brueghel I in his two paintings of *Juno in the Underworld* (Dresden, Gemäldesgalerie Alte Meister; and Brussels, Gallery Robert Finck, 1963). David's *Juno* is also related to Jan I's *Aeneas and the Sybil in Hell* (Budapest, Museum of Fine Arts; Antwerp, Baron Kronacker collection).[39] Teniers adopted his figure of Juno riding through the regions of Hell in a cart from the figure who appears in Brueghel's painting of *Juno*. The "three furies" or "fates" included in Teniers's painting were taken from the furies that can be found in the Brussels version of *Juno in the Underworld* and the Budapest painting of *Aeneas and the Sybil in Hell*. All of Jan I's paintings are populated with demons. They are also characterized by dramatic lighting. David the Younger filled his infernos with demons and also made use of dramatic lighting effects similar to those in the paintings of Jan I Brueghel.

Teniers's versions of *Latona and the Carien Peasants* (the best is owned by the Glasgow Museum and Art Gallery under the title *Latona and the Lycian Peasants*, Plate 18), were derived from Jan I's painting of *Latona and the Carien Peasants*, Plate 19. Jan I's Latona is shown accosted by the peasants, some of whom she has already transformed into frogs. A few are still wearing peasant clothes and one carries a shovel in his still human hand. Teniers also depicted some frogs still dressed as peasants. He included the frog who has not yet lost his human hands. The figure still carries a shovel just as he does in Jan I's painting. The group comprised of Latona and the two infants is placed in the same pose used by Jan I, although Teniers has once again increased the sense of drama by showing Latona with her eyes raised to heaven. He has also paid more attention to the distress of the frogs by giving them expressions that seem to indicate that they are well aware of what has happened to them.

Teniers had more than a passing interest in the works of Jan I as is shown by the number of Brueghel's works that influenced Teniers. Teniers's paintings of the *Armorer* (Chicago, Institute of Art) and the *Armorer's Shop* (Raleigh North Carolina Museum of Art) contain similar still lifes composed of cap-a-pie armor. The Chicago painting represents Archduke Albert's armor as it appeared in Jan I's painting of the *Archduke Albert's Armor* (Avignon, Musée des Beaux Arts).[40] Jan I also used armor in his *Allegory of Touch* (Madrid, Prado) and in the *Forge of Vulcan* (Rome, Doria Gallery). Teniers also painted a *Forge of Vulcan* (formerly T. Offerman collection) in which he included many pieces of armor.[41] This painting like the other armory scenes was probably also inspired by Jan I.

In her study of Flemish seventeenth-century genrists, Francine Claire Legrand credited David the Younger with the invention of the peasant kermis in which members of the bourgeoisie appear.[42] Teniers did not create this particular genre. Indeed, many members of the Brueghel school, including Jan I and Pieter II, painted kermises that include members of the upper class and nobles.[43] Again, as with his grotesques and peasant types, David the Younger was merely following a practice established by the Brueghels.

Influence of Frans Francken II. Paintings by Frans Francken II (1578-1642) were a secondary source of iconography for Teniers. Francken's contribution to the style of Teniers does not lend itself to an easy explanation since both artists appropriated some of the iconography of Pieter Brueghel I and Pieter Brueghel II. However, Francken may have transmitted some elements of Brueghelian iconography to Teniers.

That Francken was dependent upon the Brueghels is exemplified by his *Seven Acts of Mercy* of which he painted several versions based on paintings of Pieter II.[44] (Pieter II, in turn, had derived his paintings of this subject from his father's engraving of *Caritas*.) In some of his *Seven Acts of Mercy* Francken used a blind beggar, who he took from Pieter I's *The Blind Leading the Blind*. Francken's Prague *Seven Acts of Mercy* (Narodni Gallery) contains this beggar, as does a fragment owned by the Musées Royaux des Beaux-Arts, Brussels. A third version of the painting, which appeared in the 1895 Sedelmeyer sale, also showed this figure.[45] The painting from the Sedelmeyer catalog and the Brussels fragment are similar to the composition used in paintings of the *Seven Acts* by Pieter II since they depict the acts being performed in a village setting.[46] Francken included acts of mercy being performed in "cut-away" houses, which are again similar to those used by Pieter II. *The Seven Acts of Mercy* (Munich, Alte Pinakothek) provides the best evidence of Francken's dependence on the Brueghels. Francken obviously based his paintings on those of Pieter II, as did Teniers.

David the Younger painted at least seven versions of the *Seven Acts*, the best of which is the one owned by the Louvre, Plate 3. His paintings are even more closely dependent upon Pieter II than are those of Francken. Teniers placed his figures in the Louvre painting in a village setting and arranged his groups in positions within the composition that closely recall their placement in the Brueghel paintings. The act of feeding the hungry is placed in the left foreground, represented by a group of individuals distributing loaves of bread to the poor. Next to this group is a youth who is giving water to the thirsty. To the left and slightly behind the people distributing bread are those who clothe the naked. This act is performed by a young woman assisted by her servant. In the background and at the right, Teniers has depicted the visiting of the sick. The visitors are shown entering a Brueghelian "cut-away" house. The man who comforts strangers and those who visit the imprisoned are shown in the middle distance. The burial of the dead can be seen in the landscape background. Because of the close similarities in composition between Teniers's versions of the *Seven Acts* and those of Pieter Brueghel II, it would not seem too likely that Teniers derived his iconography from Francken in this case, but perhaps Francken was his inspiration to turn to the Brueghel paintings.

We know that Francken did inspire Teniers directly at times. His paintings of the *Prodigal Son* may be examples of such inspiration. David the Younger's paintings of this theme always remind one of Francken's in that the prodigal son is shown in the company of fashionable prostitutes in the paintings of both masters. While many Flemish masters used this motif, Teniers's paintings look more like Francken's than those of any other artist.

David the Younger's painting of the *Triumph of Neptune* (present whereabouts unknown) were inspired by the Francken painting of *Neptune and Amphitrite* (Madrid, Prado; Braunschweig, Herzog Anton Ulrich Museum). Francken's paintings and the photographs of the Teniers work show Neptune and Amphitrite being drawn across the waves in a cart pulled by sea beasts. Surrounding the cart are several sea nymphs, flying fish, and other aquatic creatures. All three paintings are organized along a diagonal that runs from left to right through the triumphal cart.

David the Younger painted one version of *Lot Fleeing Sodom* (private collection, United States) in which he again copied a painting by Francken. In Teniers's painting Lot and his two daughters, accompanied by an angel and a small dog, have just left the burning Sodom. Behind them in the picture's central plane stands Lot's wife, already a pillar of salt. The figures are placed in the extreme right hand corner of the scene. Lot is dressed in robes and a turban and carries a staff. The angel conducts him forward, pointing out the way. Lot's daughters walk behind him; one carries a metal pitcher and the other wears an elegant plumed hat. Teniers's figure grouping, as well as his method of representing Lot and his daughters, was borrowed from the Francken painting *The Angel Leading Lot From the Burning Sodom* (Vienna, Dorotheum, 1974). Francken depicted Lot exactly as Teniers did later: he also showed Lot being led by an angel holding his hand and pointing out the way while the daughters and a second angel follow. The only major difference between the two paintings is that the daughter with the plumed hat in the Francken painting also carries the pitcher. The positioning of the figure group is the same in both works; Francken also depicted the destruction of Sodom in the background.

Paintings by Francken played another important role in the career of David the Younger. Francken's paintings of art collections, or *kunstkamers*, were probably the most important source for Teniers's several versions of *Archduke Leopold Wilhelm's Painting Gallery* (Brussels, Paris, Munich). Reproducing the archduke's paintings was not Teniers's first venture into this category of paintings. W. Speth-Holterhoff has convincingly demonstrated that Teniers completed several gallery paintings that he purchased from the estate of Frans Francken in 1642.[47] These are the earliest known gallery paintings by Teniers. He finished Francken's canvases by filling in the paintings, sculptures, and other treasures in Francken's already-completed architectural settings. While it is known that David the Elder executed at least one kunstkamer,[48] it is here believed that David the Younger learned this particular genre from the example of Francken.

Teniers's interest in Francken again points up his eclectic nature. While the eclecticism of Teniers is especially noticeable in his early period, it is also a quality of his later years.

Stages of Stylistic Development. Teniers's early period extends from his entry into the Guild of St. Luke to about 1643. His early style is similar to that of his more familiar mature period, but it is cruder and somewhat unformed in quality. The draftsmanship of his early period is weak and less certain, his compositions are simple and not well organized, he makes less use of the diagonal as a structural principle, and his color scheme is usually quite dark. While David the Younger's brushstroke is easily identifiable at this time, his handling of paint is not as well controlled as it is later. Teniers's lack of control is especially noticeable in hands and faces, but can also be observed in his treatment of drapery.

The early-period color scheme is based primarily on harmonies of browns with some strong local color, chiefly reds and blues. This color scheme may reflect the influence of Brouwer in part, but it seems to be distinctively Teniers's, nonetheless. It is not the same as Brouwer's color scheme nor is it the same as that which Teniers himself used in his Brouwer-style paintings.

The Witch, Plate 4, provides a good example of the simple figure arrangements employed by Teniers during his early period. The painting depicts a peasant woman who has just been surprised by some unexpected results of her witchcraft. She is placed at the left of the scene. Opposite her are a number of demons and supernatural beasts that she has conjured up from the depths of the underworld. The witch kneels in a magic circle with her athame, or witch's knife, at her side. She is tying a fish to a pillow as part of her rituals, but the apparition has caused her to turn around suddenly in alarm.[49] Her obvious surprise may indicate that she has not practiced the black art long enough to have become inured to the presence of the Devil's minions. The wry humor intended in this painting is made all the more evident by the demons themselves, who do not seem particularly frightening but rather like possible figments of peasant imagination. Such humor is a characteristic of David the Younger's art, always depicting subtle but nonetheless funny situations. The presence of anthropomorphic demons, some of which are similar to peasants of Brouwer, may provide some evidence for a tentative date in the mid-1630s for this painting.

The witch and her pillow are placed on a slight diagonal that is echoed by the demons opposite her. Teniers left the center of the painting empty except for a bat and a crawling monster who have the effect of dividing the composition into halves. This enforced symmetry has created a less than satisfactory design for the painting. The eye is led directly into the center of the painting by the two diagonals, but there is no resolution of the tension produced at the point where they intersect. Teniers may have included the bat and monster in an attempt to relieve this visual strain, but these elements have had exactly the opposite effect.

The Witch is painted in a dark color scheme primarily composed of browns with some local color provided by the witch's red blouse and the blues that appear in the clothing of several demons. The sombre tonality of the painting also indicates an early date for its execution. Light enters the scene on a fairly weak diagonal from an unspecified source at the left. Some secondary illumination is provided by the witch's lamp and the candle on one demon's hat.

David the Younger's brushstroke is somewhat cruder and the paint is less carefully applied than it would be in a painting from his mature period. The draftsmanship is weak, although some areas, such as the witch's hands and features, are rather well drawn. The stylistic characteristics of this signed painting indicate that it was probably painted between Teniers's entry into the guild and 1636. By 1636 he was producing carefully finished Brouwer-style paintings that are technically more advanced than *The Witch.*

The small panel depicting *Lot and His Daughters,* Plate 20, has not been cleaned and its dark condition accounts for difficulties in determining the original color scheme. However, the painting does seem to have an overall brownish tonality with little presence of local color. It was probably painted at about the same time as *The Witch*. The setting is a cave in which Lot and the daughters have taken refuge after their flight from Sodom. The burning city may be seen in the background at the right. Lot's wife, already a pillar of salt, stands outside the entrance to the cave. A large boulder has been pressed into service as a makeshift table on which is laid a simple dinner. One daughter stands behind the table while Lot and the second daughter have seated themselves beside it.

Teniers again kept the composition simple by placing the figures in a linear arrangement. The cave walls are nothing more than a backdrop. The figures are not well related to their surroundings and the whole painting recalls the mannerist compositions of David the Elder. The painting does not contain any use of diagonals, even the light falls directly into the scene from a frontal source. Teniers did relieve the flatness of the composition somewhat by placing a still life of silver pitchers, a wine jug, and a cloth before the table. These elements too are simply arranged.

The brushstroke is somewhat obscured due to the dirty condition of the painting, but the treatment of the drapery and the drawing of the hands does not seem particularly refined. The faces of the women are especially plain. They resemble the stereotyped females of David the Elder.

The early influences of Brouwer may again be seen in yet another period painting, *The Temptations of St. Anthony*, Plate 21. St. Anthony is shown at prayer in his grotto cell kneeling at a prie-dieu fashioned from a large rock. Around him swarms a collection of demonic beasts. One demon stands at St. Anthony's left, tempting him with a large glass of wine, while others tug at the anchorite's robes. Still other evil beings fill the air with mocking prayers and harsh music. This painting is well organized by diagonals that direct the eye towards St. Anthony. The lighting is also made to further isolate the figure of the saint. The brushstroke is well controlled and the draftsmanship is noticeably improved from that of *The Witch* or *Lot*.

The color scheme is dominated by browns and greys and is reminiscent of Brouwer, as is the boer demon seated in the left hand corner of the painting. The absence of female figures may also indicate that this painting is from the early period since mature-period St. Anthonies usually contain female demons. The panel was probably painted in the late 1630s or the early 1640s.

The Prodigal Son with Prostitutes, Plate 22, was probably painted during the first half of the 1640s. The painting was executed in the dark color scheme of the early period. It contains very little local color. The draftsmanship is especially weak in the hands of most of the figures, although the general quality of drawing is good. This work illustrates the developing style of the artist. In this painting Teniers has constructed a more complex arrangement of figures than in *The Witch* or *Lot*, but the composition is still not too well controlled. The figures are grouped around a table at the right of the scene. They are arranged in a semicircle that

Teniers used to increase the depth of the painting. Despite these attempts at refining space, the eye cannot move easily from one point to another. The figures and the furnishings are strung together like a series of beads. There is not sufficient depth in the room to accommodate all the figures included.

The lighting is also rather simplistic, coming from the left and falling across the scene at a diagonal. The light was probably intended to pick out the prodigal son and the prostitute seated beside him. In the painting's present condition it does not appear that Teniers was successful with his use of light, but this appearance may be the result of the panel's dirty condition.

TENIERS'S EARLY-MATURE STYLE

Towards the end of his early period David the Younger painted works that have characteristics of both his early and mature periods. Such works were executed from about 1643 to 1646. We call this transitional phase of the artist's development his early-mature period. It is a distinct phase in that paintings from this period no longer resemble either the early or the mature styles exactly. Some works do seem more like Teniers's early style, such as *The Temptations of St. Anthony*, Plate 23, from the Museum Meyer van den Bergh, but all the paintings contain elements of the mature style. This *Temptation of St. Anthony* is primarily a tonal study in browns, but Teniers also used some grey washes in the background. Again, the color scheme reflects the influence of Brouwer. There is some limited amount of local color produced by the usual reds and blues. The color scheme of the painting appears blonder than it actually is because of the varnish coat on the panel.

In this painting David the Younger employed a technique that is stylistically between the characteristics of his early and mature periods. In some areas of still life and in the demons in the background he used a most delicate brushstroke and very thin glazes. However, his treatment of hands and facial features is still rather crude and the drawing is weak at times. Nonetheless, the use of thin glazes, thin grey overpainting, and perhaps a lighter color scheme (although this is hard to determine) does point to a date in the early-mature period for this work.

Two paintings from David the Younger's early-mature period are considered among his finest works. These are *The Parade of the St. Joris Shooting Guild* (Leningrad, The Hermitage) and *The Fat Kitchen* (Plate 7), both dated 1643. In *The St. Joris Shooting Guild*, Teniers demonstrated his ability to handle large groups of people within a painting without becoming overly repetitive or boring in composition. The painting displays technical ambiguities and a color scheme typical of this period—somewhere between the early and mature styles.

The Fat Kitchen contains the subtle play of tonalities typical of David the

Younger's mature period. It displays a degree of tonal sophistication that he rarely achieved again. The draftsmanship is also uniformly good. This too is unusual because Teniers often devoted special care in drawing to only certain selected areas of a painting. Despite these qualities, the painting is still too dark to qualify as a mature-period work. Moreoever, the draftsmanship is still slightly weak in comparison with that of the mature period.

A third painting from the early-mature period, one which is also dated 1643, is the *Kitchen Interior,* Plate 5, from the Los Angeles County Museum of Art. This painting was a collaboration between Teniers and Jan Davidsz de Heem. It seems closer to the early period of Teniers than does *The Fat Kitchen* and is discussed more extensively in Chapter 4.[50] This painting, as well as the other examples from the early-mature period, reflect the conflict of styles that David the Younger was experiencing at this time. These paintings provide us with evidence of the rapid progress that Teniers was making as an artist between 1643 and 1646. A work like *The St. Joris Shooting Guild* must have done much to enhance Teniers's reputation in Flanders and must have helped bring him to the attention of prominent patrons, such as Bishop Triest and the archduke. It must have been clear to such prospective patrons that this was an up and coming artist. The rapidity of his artistic growth was obvious in his works. By 1646 David the Younger was no longer producing the hesitant, trial and error works of his early-mature period. He had now embarked on his mature style, a syle that would not change appreciably for the rest of his life.

2 Teniers's Life and Style: 1650-1670

TENIERS'S LIFE

In 1650 David the Younger increased the scope of his activities for Archduke Leopold Wilhelm. He now entered into a position of importance in the archducal household that would insure his future for a decade to come. While he was active in Antwerp during this year, receipts from the archduke's account books show that David the Younger was working in Brussels in 1650. A receipt from the period July 1, 1650 to an unspecified date in 1651 provides evidence of David the Younger's new status at court.[1]

Extraordinarios

A David Teniers Pintor de Camera que entro un Lugar des Jan van den Heock Triscientos florines por un ano desdo primero de Julio de 1650 hasta oy dias de la fecha.

300 (signature)
David Teniers

Miscellaneous

To David Teniers Court Painter who replaced Jan van den Hoeck 300 florins for one year from the first of June 1650 to today's writing.

300 (signature)
David Teniers

This receipt is especially important because it proves that Teniers was more or less continually employed in Brussels after July 1, 1650. Further, it proves that David the Younger received the title of *pintor de camera*, or court painter, upon the death of Leopold Wilhelm's first court painter, van den Hoeck, who died in 1651.

The question of when David the Younger was made *ayuda de camera*, or gentleman of the bedchamber, has been a mystery until recently. We know

27

now that he held this position in 1658.[2] He was always mentioned as ayuda to both Leopold Wilhelm and his successor, Don Juan of Austria. If David the Younger received this honor in 1658, as the records indicate, then he could not have been directly honored by Leopold Wilhelm since he ruled only until 1656. It is likely that David the Younger received this title as a reward for his efforts in the publication of the *Theatrum Pictorum*, discussed below, but that he never actually served the Brussels court in the capacity of ayuda. The records show that he received the title in August 1658; since Don Juan left in January 1659, one suspects that this title was strictly an honor.

David the Younger was, however, the court painter to Leopold Wilhelm and as such he was called upon to record a number of important events in the life of the archduke as well as to execute several portraits of him. One such official portrait depicts the archduke at the ceremonial shooting of the popinjay outside the Church of Notre Dame du Sablon in Brussels. The canvas is dated 1652, but the work itself must have commenced sometime in 1651. An authorization deposited in the Archives de la Ville, Brussels, dated April 27, 1651, mentions this painting.[3]

Among David the Younger's more important paintings of the 1650s are the several representations of the *Painting Gallery of the Archduke Leopold Wilhelm*. Teniers frequently included himself alongside the archduke in these paintings. Occasionally he depicted other personages at court, such as Bishop Triest. During this decade David the Younger also continued to purchase paintings and tapestries for the archduke. A document deposited in the Stadsarchief, Antwerp, records a buying trip that he made on May 20, 1651.[4]

Other members of the royal entourage, among them Count Johann von Schwartzenberg, the Lord High Chamberlain, also employed David the Younger. Teniers's services to von Schwartzenberg included copying and restoring paintings and purchasing tapestries.[5]

So widespread was David the Younger's popularity that the Prince de Condé sat for his portrait in 1653 when he was in the Southern Netherlands after his defeat at the hands of Louis XIV at Arras. This portrait is preserved in the Musée Condé, Chantilly.

David the Younger was also honored with a visit by Queen Christina of Sweden when she passed through Brussels on her way to Rome in 1654. De Bie records that Christina gave Teniers a golden chain with a medal bearing her likeness as a token of her appreciation of his paintings. A similar medal was presented to Teniers by Leopold Wilhelm sometime before his departure in 1656.[6] De Bie also recorded that Teniers had painted the portrait of Charles II of England. This painting existed in the royal collections at Brussels until February of 1731, when it was destroyed in a fire.[7]

While his prosperity must have brought David the Younger much satisfaction and happiness during these years, he could not have been entirely happy. He was to lose both his young daughter, Anne Catherine, and his wife, Anna Brueghel, within two weeks in May 1656.[8]

Shortly before her death Anna Brueghel summoned the notary Kasper Baginier to witness her last testament on May 3, 1656. This document easily demonstrates the rapid growth of Teniers's wealth after nearly a decade of service to the archduke. His life as a courtier had been most profitable, for Anna herself left the sum of 3000 guldens to each of her five children plus an equal share of her jewels.[9]

The summer after Anna's death brought the departure of David the Younger's great friend and benefactor, Leopold Wilhelm, who left Brussels for Vienna in July. He was replaced by the bastard son of Philip IV, Don Juan of Austria, who made his entry into Brussels on July 16. David the Younger continued in the service of the new governor in the same capacities as he had when he served Leopold Wilhelm.

David the Younger came into legal possession of his new town house in the Rue Terarken in Brussels on October 13, 1656.[10] A week later, on October 21, he married Isabelle de Fren, daughter of the Secretary of the Council of Brabant, André de Fren, in the Church of St. Jacques sur Coudenberg.[11] Previous authors have criticized David the Younger for marrying again so soon after the death of Anna Brueghel. Van den Branden, for example, portrayed Teniers as stepping over Anna's grave on the way to the altar.[12] While it may be true that he did literally just that since Anna was buried in the Coudenberg church, Teniers's action in marrying Isabelle de Fren was not as cavalier as it might seem. Considering that he still had four children, two of whom were young at the time of their mother's death, and that he was obviously quite busy with his duties at court and with his own art business, it is little wonder that he sought someone to care for his family as quickly as possible. Such marriages, after all, were not uncommon in the seventeenth century. He had little need to marry for the dowry that a rich woman such as Isabelle might bring him. An inventory of the joint estates of David the Younger and Anna Brueghel made in December 1657 showed that their total worth was 32,170 guldens.[13]

As early as 1655 David the Younger had begun his appeal for a patent of nobility. This lengthy process gained momentum in 1657 when he made his first petition on January 16 with the support of the Antwerp City Council, which had examined his case at his request. The documents that he had compiled stated that he was of noble ancestry on both sides of his family. The ancestors of the Teniers family of Ath and Antwerp had been noblemen and his maternal grandfather, Cornelis Hendrixzone de Wilde, had been an admiral on the Scheldt. If his petitions and claims should seem insufficient, Teniers tactfully pointed out that other Antwerp artists, such as Rubens and Van Dyck, had been ennobled.[14]

The documents were presented to the Council of Brabant in Brussels for their furtherance to the king. Attached to these was a statement dated November 4, 1657, that specified that Teniers should be granted a letter patent of nobility provided that he cease to be gainfully employed as an artist or dealer.[15] Nothing came of David the Younger's first petition. In 1663 the case was again reviewed upon a second appeal by Teniers.[16]

The second appeal was accompanied by a statement from the Luxemberg king of arms, Englebert Flachio, attesting to Teniers's noble ancestry and describing the coat of arms of the Taisnière family of Ath.[17] The whole appeal was referred once again to the Council of Brabant, which debated the matter.[18] Again no patent of nobility was forthcoming from Madrid. It does seem that David the Younger received his patent some time after 1663. In 1680 Englebert Flachio again wrote to the king that he had examined the Teniers dossier. He described the family coat of arms at length and he noted that Teniers and his posterity were permitted to use this escutcheon.[19] We cannot agree with Dreher's contention that this document constitutes proof that David the Younger had actually been granted his letter patent by Philip IV before his death. The 1680 document is written in extremely bad French and is quite ambiguous. All it proves to any satisfaction is that David the Younger eventually got his letter patent. It is not clear enough to indicate *when* he received this honor.

Teniers continued to accept commissions from important clients during the reign of Don Juan of Austria. De Bie wrote that even Charles I of England called upon Teniers, [20] and von Sandrart believed that he had sold paintings directly to Philip IV himself.[21] David the Younger also continued to procure works of art for Count von Schwartzenberg, and in 1657 he purchased a number of tapestries on von Schwartzenberg's authorization.[22]

The first edition of Teniers's *Theatrum Pictorum*, the engraved catalog of 229 Italian paintings from Leopold Wilhelm's collection, was published by 1658 in Antwerp by Abraham Teniers.[23] David the Younger must have been occupied for several years in the production of the copies from which the engravings were made. The second edition of 1660 contained 244 engravings, all based on his copies. The quality of these little paintings varies considerably, but some are carefully executed and reminiscent of David the Younger's best paintings.[24] The 1660 edition of the *Theatrum Pictorum* appeared simultaneously in three languages (Flemish, French, and Spanish), all published in Antwerp by Hendrick Aertssens.[25] This is the standard edition of the catalog as it is the most complete. In 1684 a third *Theatrum Pictorum*, in Latin, as were the others, was released by H. and C. Verdussen in Antwerp. It is merely a reprint of the second edition.[26]

David the Younger devoted much attention in the mid-1660s to the founding and opening of the Antwerp Academy. He played a decisive role in obtaining the Academy's charter in 1663 and he continued to plan for its eventual opening in 1665. He was assisted in his efforts by the Antwerp Guild of St. Luke, the City Council, and the Council of Brabant. Teniers drafted a personal appeal to Philip IV, which he hoped would help persuade the king to elevate Antwerp to a status in the art world equal to that of Paris or Rome by permitting the city to establish a free public academy. The appeal was written in January 1663, but Teniers had been promoting his ideas for the academy for at least a year before that.[27] Preparations for the formal appeal to be made by the Council of Brabant and the city of Antwerp proceeded smoothly in the spring of 1663. The guild drew up a prospectus that outlined the objectives and proposed facilities of the academy. David the Younger had much to do with the contents of this document. In accordance with his own letter of appeal to the king the prospectus provided for the establishment of a free public academy of art that would offer instruction in various media. The school was to be open throughout the year. The prospectus was quite detailed and even specified the hours of classes. Provision was to be made for the hiring of two male models who would pose nude. Adequate heating and lighting were to be provided in winter for the comfort of students and models alike.[28] The academy would also contain an art gallery in which the work of students and other artists (including foreign painters) would be displayed. Teniers himself purchased some of the paintings displayed in this gallery.[29]

The Marquis of Caracena, current governor of the Southern Netherlands, took an interest in the project (perhaps at the instigation of Teniers) and gave it his official approval in the final proposal sent to Philip IV in June 1663.[30] The charter was not long in coming. In July 1663, Philip IV granted the city of Antwerp and its Guild of St. Luke the right to open their academy. The original Spanish charter was translated into Flemish and the dean of the guild, Caspar Huysbrechts, received this translated copy in Brussels in August.

The charter provided for the establishment of the academy as outlined in the prospectus, but the guild had to wait until October before any definitive steps could be taken towards opening the school. At this time the Council of Brabant officially chartered the academy in accordance with existing legal procedures. The charter issued by the Council of Brabant was written in Flemish and French and is deposited in the Stadsarchief, Antwerp.[31]

David the Younger was not the first administrator of the Antwerp Academy, as Descamps believed. Hendrick Peris was chosen to head the school at its opening. He was followed by Marten Huysbrechts and Gonzales Coques.[32] Apparently David the Younger never directed the academy. Since Teniers no longer lived in Antwerp, this position would certainly have been an imposition on his time.

David the Younger's later years seem to have been rather quiet, and on the basis of the documents that are known, we must assume that he retired from public life at the end of the reign of Don Juan of Austria. He was certainly on good terms with the Marquis of Caracena, but there are no records of any services that he may have rendered this governor.[33]

PAINTINGS: 1646-1670

As we noted earlier, David the Younger's mature style had developed by 1646 when he was painting such fully baroque mature works as the *Boers's Carouse* (London, Wallace Collection). Teniers's mature style is generally contiguous from 1646 to his last dated work in 1680. The dark colors (browns) and, to a large extent, the grey glazes of his early period had disappeared. These he replaced with a palette marked by lighter, more pastel tones. As the 1650s progressed, these tones became slightly lighter and livelier. David the Younger also improved his draftsmanship during his mature period and he paid greater attention to the execution of details with very precise brushstrokes. While some early period paintings reflect a slight trace of mannerism, the paintings of the mature period were totally devoid of any such features. Gone are the linear compositions and the ambiguities of design.

The Denial of St. Peter, Plate 24, is signed and dated 1646. It illustrates well the degree of David the Younger's stylistic development at the beginning of his mature period. The painting is in poor condition and is very dirty. In this work David the Younger used a lighter palette that still is obvious even given the dirty state of the painting. The painting, for instance, is much lighter in tonality than the *Temptations* from the Museum Meyer van den Bergh. *The Denial of St. Peter* is characterized by grey washes, but these are lighter than similar washes in paintings from the early-mature period. The brushstroke is well controlled and the paint has been laid in more smoothly. The draftsmanship is more self-assured.

A strong diagonal running from St. Peter through the group of soldiers seated at a table in the center of the scene is used to control the composition. With the exception of St. Peter all figures are dressed in contemporary costume. The card playing soldiers are grouped about the table in an arrangement that recalls Brouwer, but their faces are distinct Teniers-types.

St. Peter has just turned away from the fire to address a peasant woman who has seen him with Jesus. Although his hand is raised in a mild gesture of denial, the scene is entirely devoid of emotion. Indeed, the significance of the iconography might easily be overlooked if it were not for the presence of the cock perched on the mantlepiece above the head of the saint.

The primary light source comes from the fireplace at the left. The glow of the fire falls diagonally across the room restating the diagonal formed by the figures. A second light source is furnished by an open door in the background at right. In accordance with the understated tone of the painting, the lighting is in no sense dramatic, but merely serves as a coordinating element. Despite its stillness, the *Denial of St. Peter* is a fully baroque work.

David the Younger painted numerous versions of the *Alchemist* during his mature period. These are discussed in great detail shortly. Many of these paintings come from the early years of the mature period. Two of these paintings show changes that occurred in David's mature style towards the end of the 1640s. These changes were slight and do not constitute an argument for a second mature style, but they are noticeable. Both paintings depict serious devotees to alchemy rather than the amateurs or charlatans, known collectively as "puffers." The two paintings, owned respectively by the Herzog Anton Ulrich Museum and the Mauritshuis, seem related although the Mauritshuis version was painted later in the decade.

The *Alchemist* (Plate 25) in the Herzog Anton Ulrich Museum, Braunschweig, contains a distinguished-looking old scholar reading in his laboratory. He seems hardly aware of the activities of several assistants in the background. The alchemist is seated somewhat apart from the rest of his laboratory at a table in the right hand corner of the scene. Behind him are a row of furnaces on which three alembics, or distillation flasks, are heating. An apprentice kneels beside one furnace working a bellows. On the other side of this series of furnaces two assistants are busily preparing chemical mixtures at a small table. David the Younger evidently intended to portray a very large alchemical laboratory, the type that was often supported by seventeenth-century rulers. The composition is entirely based on diagonals and is quite competent.

David the Younger's treatment of details is especially fine in the painting. The still life elements on the alchemist's table are beautifully painted and the folded, knotted cloth placed on a stool in the center of the painting is a tour de force in itself. The cloth is executed with only one or two thin glazes. The laboratory apparatus in the background provided Teniers with an excellent opportunity to display his developing skill as a painter of delicate details. The same high-quality execution is also found in the alchemist's hands and face. This painting has been restored and this may account for the pentimento in the still life in the left foreground. The group of objects is not as well painted as is the rest of the work.

The Braunschweig *Alchemist* is primarily a study in browns with little attention given to the possibilities for tonal study offered by the steam rising from the furnaces or the glowing coals. There is some use of grey washes in the background, but these seem unusually heavy and may well be the results of restoration.

The Mauritshuis *Alchemist*, Plate 26, also depicts an old scholar conducting an experiment. He has just looked up from his reading and continues to stir the mixture in the crucible on the table in front of him. The table also contains a variety of still life painted with great delicacy in thin glazes. There is much less space in this painting than there is in the Braunschweig *Alchemist*. David the Younger repeated the same group of furnaces in both scenes but moved them forward until they are almost directly behind the alchemist's chair in the Mauritshuis version. The laboratory apparatuses in the background were also taken from the Braunschweig painting.

The Mauritshuis *Alchemist* is consciously organized by diagonals that run through the furnaces and the collection of apparatus placed on the floor in the foreground. These diagonals intersect a third diagonal formed by the books piled in front of the alchemist's table. David the Younger placed his alchemist at a point where the three diagonals meet rather than locating him slightly to one side, as he is in the earlier painting. While the organization is obviously carefully structured, the resulting composition does not appear static.

The color scheme of the Mauritshuis *Alchemist* is more typical of the artist's mature period than that of the Braunschweig painting. Teniers used the smoke and steam rising from the furnaces to create a beautiful harmony of greys and greyish blues that are blended with his more traditional brown tonalities. The subtle tones are complimented by the dull yellow in the alchemist's coat and the browns used in the fur trim on his collar and hat. The more sohisticated color scheme used in this painting indicates that it was painted at a later date than the Braunschweig *Alchemist*, probably late in the 1640s or the first part of the 1650s.

A Temptations of St. Anthony, Plate 27, owned by the Koninklijk Museum van Schoone Kunsten, Antwerp, is characterized by careful attention to the rendering of details, strong diagonals, and a well-organized composition. It also contains diagonal lighting and a good mature-period color scheme. It most likely was painted in the 1650s.

The panel is quite carefully painted with great attention given to the drawing of details and the faces of the figures. The setting is the ordinary one of a grotto in a quiet landscape. The strongly receding diagonal leading out of the cave into the landscape at the left is enhanced by a series of rock arches over the mouth of the cave. The demons include David the Younger's usual collection, but he has also included one who seems to be a minor devil. One boer-demon seated in the lower left corner looks quite like Teniers himself. If this is a self-portrait, the age of this demon would correspond to Teniers's approximate age when the work was finished.

The beautiful *St. Anthony in a Landscape* (Plate 1), owned by Frankfurt's Staedelsches Kunstinstitut, probably dates from the early 1660s.[34] The draftsmanship is of an especially high quality and the brushstrokes are carefully adjusted throughout the painting to achieve the most naturalistic depictions of rocks, sky, drapery, and anatomy. The painting was beautifully executed, but it was also rapidly painted. The background is rendered in the thinnest glazes and the brushwork in the sky indicates that it, too, was painted with great speed. This small panel is one of Teniers's most pleasing works, yet it is not well known.

David the Younger used a composition quite similar to that of the Louvre *Denial of St. Peter* in another painting in the London Wallace Collection. The painting depicts a group of soldiers gambling in a guardroom while St. Peter is liberated in the small alcove at the back. Like the *Denial of St. Peter*, this *Deliverance of St. Peter*, Plate 28, is essentially a contemporary genre scene. The miracle taking place in the background is of relatively little importance to the overall composition. Neither the light nor arrangement of figures has been devised to draw attention to this event. The figures in the foreground are arranged on a strong diagonal. This diagonal is restated by a bench in the foreground on which are placed a soldier's coat and plumed helmet. All figures are dressed in contemporary clothing except St. Peter.

David the Younger's lighting is more complicated in this work than in the earlier *Denial of St. Peter*. Once more he allowed light to fall diagonally across the scene from left to right, but he has also employed a second strong light source, which enters the scene from the front. Some further illumination is furnished by the window in St. Peter's cell and the miraculous glow of the angel.

The color scheme in the *Deliverance of St. Peter* indicates that the painting is certainly from the later years of Teniers's mature period. The palette is a subtle study of delicate reds, blues, and turquoises complimented by light grey glazes and light yellows. This painting has been relined and ironed with the result of some loss of the character of the brushstrokes. As it appears now, the handling of paint seems much too flat. Despite this appearance, the original quality of the brushstroke and the draftsmanship is still evident.

The Louvre *Seven Acts of Mercy* (Plate 3), which we noted earlier for its Brueghelian iconography, is executed in David the Younger's best mature style. The painting must be included among his finest works from any period. The color scheme is light and dominated by pastels. Teniers devoted special attention to his color harmonies in this work and it is this harmony of tones that first catches one's eye. The composition is well organized by diagonals. Most of the figures are grouped together in the foreground. This arrangement does not pose compositional problems since the figures are well placed and are coordinated by diagonal lighting. They are also well integrated with the background of the scene. The color scheme in itself helps to unify the composition further.

The painting is executed on copper, but there has been little discoloration caused by oxidation so that the original appearance of the painting has been largely retained. No part of the painting escaped Teniers the Younger's attention. Even the background landscape has been well thought out and carefully painted. Because of its excellence the Louvre *Seven Acts* stands at the apex of Teniers's mature style. It must date from the second half of the 1660s. The control exhibited in the handling of paint and in the drawing recalls Teniers's first efforts at such finesse in the *Fat Kitchen* of twenty years earlier.

By the mid-1660s David the Younger had fully refined his ability to paint delicate details. To achieve this he used thin glazes worked wet—as few as one or two on some elements of still life. The little dogs that so frequently appear in his mature-period paintings are superb examples of his fine technical ability with fragile glazes. High-quality draftsmanship and a finely developed handling of paint augmented his mature color harmonies to occasionally produce especially pleasing works like the Louvre *Seven Acts* and Frankfurt's *St. Anthony in a Landscape*. While it is true that many of David the Younger's mature period works are less well executed, it is not by these secondary works that his talents should be judged. Rather, those paintings in which Teniers appears at his best should be chosen. When he was not producing works merely for a commercial market, David the Younger could create quite acceptable and well finished paintings. Since there is such a large mature period output, only the best examples should be considered in setting up any standards of connoisseurship. It should be presumed that the artist could have created many more high-quality paintings if he had not been engaged in what was almost a mass production of paintings.

Paintings of the *Temptations of St. Anthony* constitute a major portion of the work of David the Younger. In fact these paintings make up the largest group among his religious works. Teniers painted the *Temptations* throughout his career. The earliest known dated version was produced in 1635,[35] and we know that he was still painting this theme in 1665.[36] There are undoubtedly later versions than this. These paintings combine religious themes with genre. They are strongly moralizing and contain contemporary figures. All are basically similar. The types of demons may differ and the compositions change from work to work, but St. Anthony himself always appears as an old man dressed in a black robe with the Greek letter tau on his shoulder. This letter probably symbolizes the staff that he frequently carried as a badge of his status as an abbot. It may also symbolize a pilgrim's staff.[37]

According to tradition, St. Anthony was the first hermit and the founder of ascetic monasticism. He was supposedly born at Coma or Koman in Egypt in 251. As a youth Anthony became devoted to solitude and prayer and eventually withdrew to live in tombs outside his native village. Here he was beset for many years by Satan as well as numerous demons that were sent to tempt the saint. Anthony's greatest temptation came in the form of a succubus, which Teniers represented as a fashionable prostitute with clawlike feet and a scaly tail.[38] St. Anthony continued to live this austere existence for many years despite his temptations. Legend has it that his only food was bread, water, and a little salt.[39] David the Younger usually included a flask of water or a water trough in his paintings as a reference to Anthony's asceticism. St. Anthony eventually returned to the world to found monasteries and to combat the Arian heresy. He referred to members of the Arian sect as venemous serpents.[40] Teniers may have had this in mind when he painted the snakes that frequently appear among the demons in the saint's grotto. He also included demons dressed in monk's habits and others that read mocking prayers or prayer rosaries. These figures are also probably symbolic of heretics.[41] Late in his life St. Anthony journeyed into the wilderness once again to find the hermit, St. Paul, with whom he lived until St. Paul's death. Anthony himself is said to have died in 356.[42]

Several authors contributed to the accounts of the life of St. Anthony and subsequently to his iconography. The first account of his life appeared about 356 in the writings of St. Athanasius. This account contains the story of Anthony's many encounters with demons as well as his meeting with Satan.[43] Athanasius's life of Anthony was translated into Latin by Evagius, Bishop of Antioch.[44] St. Jerome also recounted the life of Anthony in his *Vita Pauli*.[45] He seems to be the source of the story of the meeting of Anthony and Paul the Hermit and of their life together in the desert. In the thirteenth century the life of St. Anthony appeared in the *Golden Legend* of Jacobus de Varagine where it became familiar to many.[46] David the Younger may very well have developed his iconography of St. Anthony from an edition of the *Vitae patrium*, published in Antwerp in 1615 by Father Herbert Rosweyde. This anthology included both the Evagian version of the life of the saint and the *Vita Pauli* of Jerome.[47]

St. Anthony's attributes are his advanced age, a tau on a black habit, a crutch (also symbolic of age), a bell with which to dispel demons, a pig, a large staff, and fire.[48] Of these David the Younger used only Anthony's age, his habit, the tau, and the pig. The pig appears in many of the paintings as a symbol of Anthony's triumph over the temptations to lust and gluttony. David the Younger always depicted the saint in or near a grotto signifying the home he made for himself in the tombs. At times Anthony is also given a rude hut in which to live. There are a few versions of the painting that include St. Paul. This latter figure is always identified by a raven that carries a loaf of bread in its beak.[49]

Teniers's *Temptations* have some iconographic elements that are uniquely his. The demons never seem particularly horrible or frightening. At times they are even rather droll. Such is the boer demon in the Antwerp *Temptations*. St. Anthony's grotto is usually furnished with an hourglass, books, and skulls that are references to his learning and devotion to the monastic life with its ideals of endless contemplation of eternity and the frailty of human life. The flask of water or water trough also seems to be Teniers's own addition to the iconography of the saint. St. Athanasius's account noted that the Devil sent demons in the forms of bulls, lions, dragons, wolves, adders, serpents, and scorpions to torment Anthony.[50] David the Younger's paintings contain most of these creatures. The Devil appears in some versions. He usually takes his favorite form of a large black ram. Teniers also included many other animals associated with the Devil in popular culture but not mentioned in the accounts of Anthony's life. Among these are frogs, crabs, bats, owls, and *serras,* or flying fish. His most unusual imagery is found in the defecating eggs that bear the head and feet of chickens. These appear in nearly all of David the Younger's *Temptations.* They are obvious symbols of decay and defilement and were apparently invented by the artist.[51]

Demons in the paintings frequently hold just-extinguished candles. Smoke can still be seen rising from most of them. These may be a reference to the use of candles by witches. The demons who hold candles are often dressed as monks and thus may represent heretics who have smothered out the light of the true faith. The smoke rising into the air from the candles is symbolic of vanity and may refer to the foolish choices these demons made in following Satan.

Since St. Anthony was tempted to commit the sins of lust and gluttony, Teniers always included figures in the *Temptations* that symbolize one or both of these sins. The succubi are an obvious reference to Anthony's temptations to lust; other figures hold wine glasses or pipes hoping to tempt him into further excesses.

David the Younger apparently painted only one *Temptations* in which the saint is tempted by personifications of all the "Seven Deadly Sins." This is *The Temptations* from the Prado, already discussed as an example of Brueghelian iconography. There is another painting attributed to him (present whereabouts unknown) in which Anthony is tempted by Anger, Avarice, Gluttony, and Lust. The allegorical figures in this painting are similar to those in the Prado painting.[52] Perhaps this was a study for the Prado *Temptations.* Because of its unusual iconography, the Prado *Temptations* must have been executed for a specific commission.

In contrast to his paintings of the *Temptations of St. Anthony,* David the Younger's few versions of *Sts. Anthony and Paul* belong to another entirely different category of purely religious paintings. They are quieter and more introspective works, reflecting the meditative atmosphere of the saints' lives. They rarely contain genre elements, nor are they moralizing in tone.

While there are between one and two hundred paintings of the *Temptations of St. Anthony* by Teniers, there are about twice as many of the *Alchemist.* This was the artist's favorite theme after his peasant genres. He returned to it again and again during his mature period. David the Younger might naturally have become interested in painting alchemists. Their activities were of interest to him professionally. Many artist's pigments and glazes used in the seventeenth century were produced by none other than alchemical methods. For example, a recipe for the refining of ivory black included salt, *Lutum sapientiae,* and ivory black all heated in a well closed container (an alembic?). *Lutum sapientiae* was a typical alchemist's concoction of clay, horse dung, finely chopped straw or finely ground glass, chalk, brick dust, lead white, and egg white.[53] It is most likely that Teniers visited alchemical laboratories, perhaps even frequently, to purchase pigments. Furthermore, if he prepared his own pigments at home, he undoubtedly engaged in alchemy himself.

Alchemical laboratories must also have been of artistic, perhaps aesthetic, interest to David the Younger. Their rooms were filled with apparatus and frequently enveloped in an atmosphere of smoke and steam that presented him with ample possibilities for depicting the delicate still lives and the subtle harmonies of color that he so enjoyed. Furthermore, the subject of alchemy must have been quite popular with the buying public because of the widespread public interest in the subject. This would account for Teniers's many versions of the theme of the *Alchemist*. With the exceptions of a few satires the majority of David the Younger's alchemists may be considered simply as observations of one phase of seventeenth-century science. The popularity of alchemy in the seventeenth century is almost astonishing. Studies of the number of alchemical treatises published between 1500 and 1700 reveal that alchemical literature reached a peak of popularity about 1600, but many works were published during the course of the seventeenth century as well.[54] Kurt K. Doeber has compiled a list of over one hundred books on alchemy published in that century, many being published in Antwerp and Brussels.[55] Alchemy aroused so much public interest that it even became a theme in literature and drama. It attracted the interest of rulers who hoped to use it to increase their personal fortunes. Far from an idealistic study practiced only by dreamers and charlatans, alchemy constituted an integral part of seventeenth-century scientific thought and thus attracted some of the finest minds of the period.

Frequently little distinction was made between alchemy, chemistry, and medicine. The preparation of artist's pigments, mentioned earlier, is a case in point. Many scientists discussed the three disciplines simultaneously in their writings. For example, Phillip Muller's *Chemical Miracles and Medical Mysteries*, published in 1610 and dedicated to Archduke Maximilian II of Austria (who was himself a devotee of alchemy), contained chapters on chemistry (alchemy) and medicine.[56] Johannes Glauber, the Dutch chemist who discovered the cathartic salts that bear his name, wrote numerous texts that treat the subjects of medicine, chemistry, and alchemy all at the same time.[57]

With so much time devoted to alchemy by the educated and ignorant alike, it is not surprising that David the Younger found the depiction of alchemists both interesting and lucrative. Furthermore, for an artist who was certainly interested in making money, these paintings represented his own personal philosophers' stone, a catalyst for transmuting base materials into gold.

Teniers always depicted his alchemists studying or devising experiments in their laboratories. Most are middle-aged. Some work in large laboratories of the type established by rulers like Archduke Maximilian, while others conduct their experiments in more humble surroundings suggestive of laboratories that they might have set up in their own homes. David the Younger's paintings of alchemists can always be identified (and thereby separated from his frequent paintings of village doctors and old scholars) by the presence of certain pieces of laboratory apparatus which were indispensable to an alchemical operation. All the paintings of alchemists contain either crucibles, alembics (distillation flasks), or athanors (large metal furnaces that resemble stoves). Most of the paintings contain several of these pieces of apparatus, although the presence of any one object is sufficient to identify the subject as alchemy. Teniers alchemists were always surrounded by many books, hourglasses, globes, and other articles suggestive of erudition. Including such articles increased the accuracy of the paintings, since alchemy was a highly speculative science whose devotees spent much of their time reading and studying one another's treatises. Some of these books also contained formulas. We know from the study of engravings of alchemical apparatus that the other objects that Teniers included in his paintings (such as tongs, measuring devices, flasks, and the like) were quite accurately represented. The alchemical paintings of David the Younger may thus be considered as authentic views of seventeenth-century alchemy. They are frequently used today as illustrations in texts on the history of science.

Émile Grillot de Givry noted in his history of alchemy and alchemical symbolism that Teniers seemed to have two opposing comments to make on the subject. David the Younger painted many reputable alchemists (his self-portrait in Munich is an example), but he also represented the fools and the charlatans known as "puffers."[58] However, his paintings satirizing alchemists are actually few in number. His most satirical painting of alchemy survives only in an engraving by Le Bas, entitled *The Pleasure of Fools*.[59] This depicts an ape who is busily working a bellows under a crucible. Teniers's other satires of alchemy contain comments far less critical than this. Even *The Pleasure of Fools* must be considered in the light of David the Younger's other *singeries* (paintings of apes). He also painted ape-sculptors and ape-painters. It is not likely that he would have heaped such great scorn on his own profession.[60] These paintings are no more critical than his many scenes of singing cats and dogs or apes smoking in guard rooms. They all seem characterized by a good-natured humor that does not admit strong criticism. David the Younger's satires of alchemy never reached the degree of biting sarcasm found in Pieter Brueghel I's famous engraving of *The Alchemist*. The majority of Teniers's alchemists appear as serious scholars rather than fools or dishonest men. The nature of the type of satire in which he did engage in alchemical paintings may be seen in two of his more satirical *Alchemists*. An *Alchemist*, known only from an engraving by Aliamet (Plate 29), depicts a very earnest youth working in a laboratory. Several assistants are also seen preparing substances at a table in the background. This *Alchemist* would be indistinguishable from Teniers's other paintings of serious scholars if it were not for the presence of one extremely important iconographical element that identifies the scene as one of satire: a small owl has perched on the shutter above the alchemist's furnace. Its presence is sufficient to change the whole meaning of the painting. Owls frequently appeared as symbols of evil, folly, or stupidity in seventeenth-century Netherlands and the presence of this small owl indicates that foolish or dishonest activities are happening under its gaze. The popular associations of the owl with evil or folly are reflected in several Dutch proverbs. The owl's nocturnal habits and his preference for dark places in which to roost gave rise to the proverb, "This is a real nest of owls," meaning any place characterized by darkness, dirt, and decay. The sense of the proverb may be expanded to include places in which evil may easily happen.[61] Perhaps because of its clumsy mode of flight, the owl was also believed to be stupid. The proverb,"*Zo dom als een uil*," literally "as stupid as an owl," reflects this belief.[62] The owl's clumsy flight was probably the source of a second proverb, "*zo dronken als een uil*," "as drunk as an owl." Owls thus were associated with the foolish actions of the drunkard, not to mention the evil connotations attached to excessive drinking.[63] In addition to its relationship to evil, foolishness, and stupidity, the owl was also more directly symbolic of several of the "Seven Deadly Sins," including pride and envy. The *Dialogus creaturum*, published in Gouda in 1480, relates the legend of the owl's great envy of the eagle, the prince of birds. So envious did the owl become that he finally led a rebellion against the eagle. The rebellion (an obvious parallel to the story of Lucifer) caused other birds to turn against the owl forever. In his study of a Bosch drawing of *Owls in a Tree*, Jacob Rosenberg further associated the owl with the sin of greed. He believed that Bosch intended the owls and other birds that appear in this drawing to represent the evil inherent in all nature, including man.[64]

The small owl that Teniers included in his *Alchemist* might easily have symbolized several of the weaknesses and evil traits found in the personality of the puffer. The greed that led such men to try to transmute base metals into gold, their usual stupidity, and the inevitable folly of their experiments all find expression in the owl perched over the alchemist's furnace. The owl was also related to an individual who had an inflated opinion of himself. The proverb, "*ieder meent dat zijn uil een valk is*," or "everyone believes his owl is a falcon," refers to those who have overestimated themselves in some way.[65] Certainly such a sense of personal importance and pride in one's intelligence would have characterized a puffer.

While it is true that owls were also associated with wisdom (as attributes of Athena), it is not the case that David the Younger intended his owl in the *Alchemist* to represent wisdom. He used owls exclusively as symbols of evil, stupidity, or folly. He painted no known allegories of wisdom in which owls appear; there are no paintings of scholar-saints in which he included owls as anythig but evil creatures. Several *Temptations of St. Anthony* contain owls, but these are always included among the other demonic beasts accosting the saint. Owls also appear among the monsters in such paintings as *Dives in Hell*. Teniers also used them in many of his interior scenes of peasants drinking and carousing in taverns.

A second *Alchemist* from the Fine Arts Gallery of San Diego, Plate 30, contains another satire of alchemy less subtle than that of the Aliamet engraving. The painting shows an old alchemist seated before a table on which are a large pile of books. He holds a flask whose contents he studies carefully. Behind him stands a sad-looking woman. She has evidently been weeping and is still wiping her eyes in an effort to regain her composure. She is the alchemist's wife, a motif that Teniers must have borrowed from the sorrowful wife in the Brueghel engraving of *The Alchemist*. This alchemist's wife is also a symbol of the effects of the puffer's insatiable desire for gold that has caused him to exhaust the family's total fortune in his attempts to find the secret of the philosopher's stone. Although his wife may weep and protest her husband's foolishness, she has not been able to prevent him from practicing alchemy. Indeed, he continues to experiment as she weeps and is unaware of the misery he is causing. A Teniers painting that depicts a scene similar to this was engraved by Le Bas as *Le Chymiste*. John Read, in one of his several works on alchemy, noted that *Le Chymiste* actually portrayed a village doctor attending to his patient.[66] If the engraving was made after the San Diego painting or one similar to it, then the engraving also represents an alchemist. The painting contains several alembics among the equipment shown and therefore must be an *Alchemist* rather than a *Village Doctor*. Teniers painted several other *Alchemists* in which he used the motif of the weeping wife, but this motif was relatively uncommon in his work. That none of these paintings had been traditionally considered a *Village Doctor* further substantiates our contention that the San Diego painting has been correctly identified.[67]

Although most of his *Alchemists* date from David the Younger's mature period, he painted them throughout his career. The *Alchemist*, dated 1680, in the Schleissheim Gallery is a self-portrait of Teniers and is the last dated work we know. Another *Alchemist*, which must be dated in the 1670s or the 1680s on the basis of style, is owned by the Prado. We will discuss these paintings further in our discussion of late paintings in Chapter 3.

David the Younger represented witches on fewer occasions than he did alchemists, but his paintings of witches reveal that he was quite familiar with the whole range of satanic practices and the current beliefs about witchcraft. As a good Catholic, he probably believed in the existence of witches and demons. He must have shared this belief with the general populace of Flanders as occurrences of witchcraft were quite frequent in the seventeenth century. The activities of witches aroused much suspicion and interest throughout the Southern Netherlands during this century. At Valenciennes one hundred and eighty-three persons were executed as witches between 1595 and 1614.[68] Thirty-three individuals were accused in Entre-Sambre-et Meuse in 1616.[69] So frequent were the occurrences of witch-craft in Ghent that warnings of excommunication of witches were published several times a year on a regular basis beginning in 1632.[70] David the Younger might easily have heard accounts or have attended witch trials as thirty-three witches were put to death in Malines between 1544 and 1663.[71] David the Younger was in Malines frequently as his country residence was situated on the outskirts of this town. He might also have learned of the practices of witches from sermons or from any of several treatises on witch-craft published during the century. These were regularly used as guides for the identification of witches by exorcists and those who presided over witch trials.[72] Descriptions of rites contained in these books certainly became parts of sermons and popular beliefs.

Most of Teniers's paintings of witches were executed in the same serious vein as his paintings of alchemy. A few contain some slightly humorous satire, but generally Teniers took his witches seriously. This may have been due to a sincere belief in such creatures on his part. He knew well the activities of witches. The paintings are always iconographically correct in their representations of satanic ceremonies and they frequently depict several of these activities taking place at once. In general, Teniers avoided the more gruesome aspects of witchcraft so that his paintings do not show witches exhuming corpses, for example, or boiling infants in cauldrons.

The Witch (Plate 4) is unusual for its humorous treatment of the subject. The painting contains only a few identifiable pieces of witch's parapher-nalia, but these are sufficient for conjuring up the demons that have appeared in the scene. The witch kneels in a magic circle that she has inscribed on the floor with her athame, or witch's knife. A circle produced in this manner is absolutely necessary for conjuring a demon. Teniers placed a small stone inside the circle. Perhaps his witch intended to summon the demon Frimost, who only appeared on Tuesday night upon the pledge of a pebble found earlier during the day.[73] The fish that she has tied to a pillow does not seem to belong to the standard repertoire of occult devices; it is a reference, as discussed earlier, to the Flemish proverb that describes a woman of no small temper and capabilities who could tie the Devil to a pillow. While David the Younger has suggested to his viewers that this is a femme formidable—a true "Dulle Griet,"—he has also depicted her fright at the appearance of a group of demons who hardly seem monstrous, but are almost amusing. The painting may actually depict an aggressive woman whose self-confidence has taken her too far rather than an actual instance of witchcraft.[74]

The *Incantation Scene*, Plate 31, easily demonstrates Teniers's familiarity with the activities and iconography of witches. Strictly speaking, the title is inaccurate in that what is actually shown is a preparation for a sabbat. The scene takes place in a room in which several witches are engaged in preparing the "food" to be served at their sabbat, conjuring up demons who will probably accompany them, and preparing themselves to fly with the aid of magic ointment.[75] While sabbats usually took place out-of-doors, it was not uncommon for witches to meet in each other's homes to conduct rituals.[76] This is what is seen here. Any place in which witches congregated was characterized by smoke, wind, and darkness.[77] Such is the atmosphere of this painting. The old witch who stirs her cauldron in the background is surrounded by several demons, including a few fish flying through the air above her. These are serras, mythical flying fish, associated with the Devil.[78] The winds of evil that howl around her have caused her hair to stand straight out in front of her head. This was a common means of demonstrating the supernatural powers of witches. David the Younger used this same motif in another painting of a witch preparing her brew owned by the Hamburg Kunsthalle.

While their manner of locomotion varied, all witches flew to their sabbats. Some were transported by demons, others changed themselves into animals, and still others flew on the more familiar broomsticks. This last group used a magic ointment made from various noxious herbs and the fat of unbaptised infants to enable them to fly.[79] In *Incantation* Teniers has shown one witch who has already changed into a beast with the hind quarters of a horse and a raccoon's tail and another, mounted on her broomstick, who is being anointed with the ointment of flight. Both will soon fly away up the chimney and journey to their sabbat.

Candles were important in any witch's rituals and these are included in *Incantation* along with candalabra made from animal paws.[80] The witches used an athame to draw a magic circle on the floor in the foreground. In this circle they have placed a skull and crossbones topped with a small vase of flowers. The flowers were probably added as a decorative element rather than as an integral part of the ceremonies that Teniers depicted.

Two witches are seated at a table in the foreground of this painting reading from a book of charms and incantations. Such "black books," or *grimoires,* were indispensable to witches. They contained prayers to the Devil, various spells, and occasionally the names of the members of a coven.[81] It is probably these witches who have conjured up the demons that appear at the left, although these creatures may have been sent to assist the witches in their rituals. The younger witch has removed her shoes, probably in deference to the sacred activities that are taking place but also in preparation for her impending flight. On the table before her is a small jar which may contain magic ointment. She seems entirely undisturbed by the demons who have gathered before her. Indeed, she may have been the one who summoned them as the younger members of a coven usually had the duty of reciting all the spells at any gathering.[82] While the young witch is somewhat coarse and evil-looking, her face bears the unmistakable features of Anna Brueghel. As she did on so many occasions, David's wife served as a model for this painting.

David the Younger obviously intended *The Incantation* as a straight-forward representation of the activities of sorceresses, one that might inspire fear and dread in its viewers. The Devil himself has appeared in one of his favorite forms, that of a large black ram, in the fireplace in the background.

The *Incantation* somewhat resembles Frans Francken II's *Assembly of Witches* (Vienna, Kunsthistorisches Museum), although David the Younger probably did not intend to copy the Francken painting. Both paintings show young and old witches consulting over grimoires, witches stirring cauldrons, nude witches being anointed with magic flying ointment, magic circles, athames, skulls and crossbones, candalabras made from animal paws, and numerous demons. Teniers's painting is much less theatrical than Francken's, but both seem to have been designed to create accurate accounts of witches' rituals. Both are in close iconographic agreement with the practices outlined in the *Compendium Maleficarum* and other similar treatises. As with his paintings of alchemists, David the Younger's paintings of witches may also be considered as records of a part of the culture of seventeenth-century Flanders that he so carefully described.

During the 1650s David the Younger also worked on the several hundred small copies for the *Theatrum Pictorum*. These were strictly intended for the use of the engravers. Most of these were painted on panels, although it is not unknown to find a copy painted on canvas. The works seem to be singular examples in that Teniers painted only one copy per painting in the archduke's collection. There is one exception, however: the *Good Samaritan* by Bassano was copied twice. The copies are found today in the collections of the Metropolitan Museum of Art and of Count Antoine Seilern. Both are almost exactly alike in the arrangement of figures and the attention paid to quality. The Metropolitan Museum's copy may be slightly more finished and perhaps it was this painting that the engravers used.

Despite the fact that the copies were sometimes not executed with great care, they always retain features of David the Younger's mature style. They are useful as studies of the techniques he employed when imitating works by other masters and when working rapidly. These small paintings were obviously produced with great speed.

The Metropolitan Museum version of the *Good Samaritan*, Plate 32, is especially well painted. The panel has been finished with almost as much care as Teniers devoted to his own larger paintings. The painting has been cleaned recently and is in good condition. The color scheme is very delicate and is dominated by light browns, greens, pinks, and greys. Much attention was given to details that need not have been painted so carefully for a mere copy. The little panel is well enough executed to stand as an individual painting.

An example of a copy in which David the Younger tried to sublimate his personal style to that of the artist he was copying (Titian) is the *Madonna of the Cherries* (Plate 33). This painting is owned by the Wallace Collection, London. It is painted on canvas and has apparently been ironed at some time as the paint seems slightly flattened. Some details, such as the cherries and the hands of the figures, are still well preserved. David the Younger adhered so closely to Titian's style that the figures have little about them that recalls his own technique. The brushstroke in the drapery is the most obvious evidence of his hand.

Another painting from the Wallace Collection is a copy of Bassano's *Ascension*. This provides a good example of a copy on which David the Younger spent very little effort. Only the figures in the foreground have received any real attention. The background is painted in only thin glazes and the figure of Christ is poorly handled. The figures themselves all resemble Teniers types and have little about them that recalls Bassano. The best areas in the painting are found in the hands of the foreground figures.

Teniers probably attempted to reproduce more accurately works that he considered valuable or that were the archduke's favorites. This would account for the discrepancies in the quality of the copies. No work is ever a slavish imitation of the style of any master and while the paintings vary considerably, they reveal that David the Younger could assimilate another's style quite readily. The archduke must have attached much significance to the *Theatrum Pictorum* since he instructed his own court painter to create the copies. Almost any artist could have come in and have created acceptable copies for engravers to use. There was no need to call in Teniers. Perhaps the importance of the catalog and Teniers's excellent job in preparing it explain why he was granted his honor of ayuda de camera. It is here believed that his honor was a well-deserved reward.

3 Teniers's Life and Style: 1670-1690

TENIERS'S LIFE

We know almost nothing about David the Younger's activities during the 1670s. With the exception of a few paintings from this decade, which prove that he was still painting, the records are silent. This is in keeping with the quiet nature of his later years.

The last decade of his life was filled with conflicts and sorrow. A clear picture of what actually transpired during these years has not emerged, But David the Younger became embroiled in a long-lasting legal dispute with his children during the early 1680s. The first records of this dispute come from 1683, although we may presume that the conflict began several years before, perhaps even shortly after the death of Anna Brueghel in 1656. Teniers was reluctant to pay Anna's children the inheritance left them in her testament of 1656. Since the estate was to have been equally divided among the four remaining children, the inheritance must have been intended to be in the form of partial compensations or interest on the value of the estate until David the Younger himself should die. This is indicated in letters written by David the Younger to his sons, David III and Leopold.[1]

Anna's children, led by David III and Leopold, claimed that their stepmother was alienating their father from them, presumably in favor of herself and her own children. David III filed suit for the inheritances sometime in 1683. The charges against David the Younger appear in a statement notarized by Ferdinand Du Mont in Brussels during this year.[2]

If he were reluctant to pay, David the Younger was equally reluctant to engage in lawsuits with his own children. In March 1683 he wrote two notarized letters to David III and Leopold in which he promised to pay the claims of all his children. These letters contain his protests that the concessions and interests that he would have to pay were too costly for a man of his income.

Soo pretendere ick by deser schrifte U. L. door notaris ende twee getuyghen geinsumeert dat U. L. voor syne portie sult hebben juste afcortinghe to doen . . . protestere ick ten hoochten van schaede ende interest.[3]

So I promise you by this letter before a notary and two witnesses assembled that you shall have justice for your portions paid on account (or paid in partial payments) . . . I protest to the high amount of the concessions and interests.

The existing records of the case do not provide any definite answers to the question of why David the Younger had not previously settled Anna Brueghel's estate. Perhaps he had indeed suffered the financial difficulties the letters seem to indicate.[4] It may also be that Isabelle de Fren had indeed turned him away from the children of Anna Brueghel. The case continued into May 1684 when a partial settlement was made in favor of the claims of David III and Antoine Teniers. In June a second settlement was reached in favor of Leopold and Corneille.[5]

The ill feelings caused by these conflicts must have been difficult for Teniers to bear. Added to his grief were the deaths of Leopold on December 6, 1684,[6] and of David III on February 10, 1685.[7] Teniers also lost his second wife about this time. De Pauw stated that Isabelle de Fren died in 1686, but this is by no means a certain date.[8] Her tombstone was inscribed "Isabelle de Fren, Huysvrouwe van den Heere David Teniers," indicating that she did die before her husband.[9]

It is not clear how much lasting damage his children's lawsuits had on David the Younger's mental condition. His letters to Leopold and David III are primarily legalistic in nature and are marked by a tone of resignation, but they do not betray anger or bitterness. No other statements that might indicate how Teniers felt about the suits have come to light. Apparently David the Younger did not draft a last testament, which might have reflected his mood prior to his death. All that is certain is that he was mentally alert in his late seventies and quite capable of handling his own affairs with ease and dignity. Several nineteenth-century Belgian scholars, including Galesloot and van Lerius, discussed whether Teniers had been so deeply embittered by his children's lawsuits that he might have taken his life. This discussion probably arose because neither the site of Teniers's grave nor any record of his burial has been found.[10] It is unlikely that Teniers committed suicide. There is nothing to indicate suicidal despondency in the letters to his sons. In addition, in the midst of this dreadful conflict Teniers was still actively engaging in his everyday dealings in art.

Teniers came into conflict with the Brussels guild in 1683 when the guild brought suit to prevent him from holding a public sale of paintings in his home in the Rue Terarken. There is nothing to indicate that Teniers was anything but his usual self during the course of this suit. Indeed, Galesloot, who researched the case more thoroughly than anyone else, characterized

Teniers's activities as those of an ultimate egoist who expected the guild to grant him special privileges. Galesloot also presumed that Teniers wished to hold this sale in order to obtain enough money to pay off his children.[11] Whatever his motives, Teniers proposed a sale of Flemish and Italian paintings to take place on July 18, 1683. The guild filed suit on July 13, stating that such a sale by an individual artist was prohibited by city ordinance and by guild rules. David the Younger cited his presumed right to engage in free enterprise (a surprisingly modern concept!) and claimed that the guild had no right to restrict sales by individuals since other guilds permitted their members to engage in similar activities. The guild relented and broke off its suit, and presumably the sale took place.[12] Teniers's protestations seem angry and spirited, but they do not sound like those of a man rendered so unstable by depression that he would soon take his life.

If David the Younger had committed suicide, it seems likely that the act would have received more notoriety than his natural death. And yet Houbraken's life of Teniers, the first published after he died, mentions nothing of a suicide. In fact, Houbraken did not even publish a date of death.

David the Younger died on April 25, 1690, at the age of seventy-nine. He was not buried with the honors that might have befitted the ayuda de camera of Leopold Wilhelm and Don Juan of Austria. Perhaps this was due to the retirement of his last years. These years of Teniers's life are filled with many unanswered questions. Certainly he continued to paint and sell his works. He also continued to deal in art. But he no longer had prominent patrons or a voice in the Brussels court. His technique did not deteriorate appreciably during these years, but it is possible that his style merely went out of fashion by the 1680s. Perhaps he did become as irascible as Galesloot suggested. After so many years as a public figure and highly prolific artist he probably just got tired of so much activity. Teniers did not keep journals or leave letters in which he expressed his feelings about anything, let alone old age and retirement. Because of this, his last years may always be shrouded in mystery.

Much has been written recently about the presumed personality of David the Younger. He strikes this author as a rather dull, "nine-to-five" working man. He was undoubtedly ambitious and pursued fame and the gathering of money assiduously, but we do not think of him as a flamboyant and exciting personality as Rubens was. He was a working artist, a member of a family trade—not a bohemian. In fact, one suspects that the notion of an artist as a maverick in society would have distressed Teniers considerably. Bohemians, after all, would not have made enough money to support eleven children and two wives. It is only since the phenomenon of the impressionists, a scant one hundred years ago, that artists have disdained to consider themselves as (normal) working members of society. A man such as Teniers falls into the modern category of a commercial artist, one who creates what people want to buy. While some might consider that this category was not fit place for an artist to be, it was what artists were in the seventeenth century. It was not disgraceful for Teniers to paint several thousand paintings and then proceed to sell them. This meant he was a success—not a hack—to his contemporaries.

THE LATE WORKS

David the Younger's technique and color scheme changed only slightly during the last two decades of his life. We know of only a few paintings that can be reliably dated from this period, but these indicate no substantial changes in style. There is no late period as such. The late paintings show a slightly weakened diagonal structure, somewhat lighter colors, but a continuing high quality of brushwork and draftsmanship. There are really few changes from the style of paintings of the 1660s. We know that David continued to paint, but it would seem that he no longer produced the great volume of paintings that he had earlier.

Three paintings will serve as examples of such refinements as David the Younger did make towards the end of his life.[13] The themes continued to be the same. During the mid-1670s David collaborated with Gautier Guysaerts on a series of nineteen paintings of portraits in flower garlands, the so-called *Nineteen Martyrs of Gorcum*.[14] These were a group of Catholic clergy killed during the Protestant fury of the Netherlands revolt. One of these panels survives, the *Blessed Jan van Weert*, Plate 34.[15] It was most likely painted in or slightly after 1675 since the portrait bears the inscription, "B. Hier. van Weert." Jan van Weert was beatified in 1675 and this inscription indicates that the painting was executed after his beatification.[16] The painting also bears the signature of Fr. G. Guysaerts and the monogram of David the Younger. Guysaerts was a specialist in flower pieces who entered the Franciscan order at Malines in 1674. The series of paintings was supposedly executed at the request of Tenier's son, Antoine, who was a recollect (a type of Franciscan friar) at Malines.[17] Because this panel bears a reliable date, ante quem, it is especially important in documenting both David the Younger's activities in the 1670s and in indicating the state of skill that he could muster in his sixties. There seems to be no appreciable diminution of quality in this work.

Two versions of the alchemist were also painted late in Teniers's life. The *Alchemist* in the Prado, Plate 35, which is signed but not dated, most likely dates from the 1670s. It seems closely related in style to the *Alchemist* from the Schleissheim Gallery. This painting is dated 1680 (Plate 6).

An old alchemist stands working a bellows at a furnace in the left foreground. Behind him can be seen another furnace before which several assistants are seated. The scene is filled with alchemical apparatus including a large athanor, or portable stove, placed in the left corner of the painting. Light enters the scene from two windows in the left side of the room. The composition is similar to that of the Schleissheim Gallery *Alchemist;* it is organized with weak diagonals that produce a somewhat cluttered appearance. In both paintings Teniers included many still life elements that provided him with opportunities to paint details with delicate glazes. The Prado painting is dirty and while this probably obscures some of the details, David the Younger's handling of paint still impresses one with its competence. The color scheme is a study of pinks and greens. The alchemist is dressed in a green robe that is contrasted with the pinks used in the clothing of the assistants. There is almost no use of grey glazes in the painting. The color scheme provides another link between this work and the Schleissheim *Alchemist,* which also contains a limited palette based on greens with almost no greys.

The similarities between the Prado and Schleissheim paintings do seem to provide evidence for the assignment of a late date to the Prado painting. These two works may indicate that David the Younger had begun to modify his palette somewhat. If this is the case, it is the only important change that took place in the style of the elderly Teniers.

An examination of the mature and late work of David Teniers the Younger leads us to the question, was David the Younger a baroque master? His professional career easily encompasses most of the period of the Flemish high baroque yet his style seems much different from that of Rubens or Van Dyck. David the Younger's style is quieter in color and lighting. His compositions are more restrained and less theatrical than those of the high baroque. While we know that there was almost no direct influence on David the Younger from Rubens or Van Dyck, there was probably some indirect influence. There are occasional paintings in which David the Younger does seem to approach the high baroque, such as the *Assumption* (Plate 36) in the *Mysteries of the Rosary* series. But even a work such as this falls far short of the style. Instead of appearing properly ecstatic and pious, the Virgin looks bored. The composition seems awkward and the colors are far too delicate. It seems quite clear that David the Younger may not be considered a *high baroque* master in the sense of Rubens or Van Dyck, but the question still remains, was he baroque in any sense?

To answer this question we must return to the origins of David the Younger's style. David the Elder was first of all a mannerist. Yet David the Younger's style is never manneristic. There is only a slight amount of influence in his style which we may attribute to David the Elder. Further, we know that David the Elder himself was influenced by his son's mature period style.

It may seem quite obvious that we cannot seek our explanation in the styles of Rubens and Van Dyck. After all, we have just stated that David the Younger was littled affected by these men in a direct sense. Yet this is not an adequate solution. There is much in David the Younger's style that may at least be *compared* to the high baroque. While his overall effect is quite different, his use of dramatic lighting and color, of multiple glazes and painterly effects, of diagonals, and of the feeling of the momentary all derive from high baroque. It may also be noted that his paintings reflect a typical baroque love for the exotic and the didactic. His many paintings of alchemists, witches, demons, and fortune tellers indicate that he was certainly interested in the bizarre and the unusual. Many of his religious paintings are actually religious genre studies that were readily understandable and quite moralizing in nature. Themes such as the *Prodigal Son*, the *Temptations of St. Anthony,* and the *Rich Man in Hell* all had clear messages for the viewer. The use of everyday figures must have made their effect all the more immediate. In this sense David the Younger's style was influenced by counter-Reformation aesthetics and related to the high baroque.

It would seem best to place David the Younger among those artists of the seventeenth century whose style was a diminished version of the high baroque of Rubens and Van Dyck. Teniers's quiet baroque verges on classicism in some instances. It is much more commonplace among seventeenth-century Flemish artists to find this type of baroque rather than the more flamboyant high baroque style. Most artists could not, or did not care to, paint in such a style. It is important to remember in this connection that most of David the Younger's paintings were cabinet pieces. The nature of his patronage (which was largely from the bourgeois class) accounts for much of the quieter tone in his work. There was no great demand among his patrons for full-blown, high baroque art. Even his works for Archduke Leopold Wilhelm were executed in this quiet baroque style.

While David the Younger's style may have been conditioned by his patrons, this factor alone does not provide an answer as to why his style developed as it did. David the Younger's quiet baroque style probably was derived in part from the influences of Adriaen Brouwer and Jan Brueghel I. His use of glazes and painterly effects most certainly derives at least in part from Brouwer's techniques. From Jan Brueghel I came some of David's love for bizarre and exotic subjects. Brueghel's use of light and decorative color, as well as his fragile nuances of landscape, certainly had its influence in the landscapes of David the Younger.

Here we must also mention the paintings of two other masters of baroque landscape. David the Younger collaborated with both Jacques d'Arthois and Lucas van Uden. Their landscapes have much in common with those of Teniers, and they influenced his mature landscape style. These collaborations and their resultant influences will be discussed in Chapter 4.

David the Younger may be included among those Flemish masters of the seventeenth century whose style anticipates rococo. Again, there is a parallel to the styles of Rubens and Van Dyck.[18] David the Younger's light color schemes, his rather delicate and decorative treatment of landscape, and the nonconsequential themes of his genres look forward to the decorative cabinet art of the eighteenth century. These qualities may account for his great popularity after 1700. His art was well received by eighteenth-century critics and collectors. The large number of eighteenth-century followers of Teniers, as well as an equally large number of forgers, attest to this continuing popularity. In one sense the style of David the Younger may be seen as an aesthetic bridge between the two centuries.

4 Teniers's Students, Collaborators, and Followers

This chapter is by no means an exhaustive list of all the artists who at some time copied David the Younger or painted a work in a category frequently used by him. Instead, this discussion is confined to artists who were directly influenced by David the Younger or whose works bear the obvious stamp of his style. Without such limitations a discussion of David the Younger's followers would go on forever. Therefore, this chapter is primarily concerned with seventeenth-century artists, although we have included some eighteenth-century masters who were influenced by David the Younger, as well. Some of these men copied Teniers frequently, while in the case of others Teniers's influence may be represented by one or two paintings only. This limited discussion leaves out entirely the great number of anonymous painters who created works in David the Younger's style. Such paintings were frequently forgeries and present a discouraging prospect of lengthy work to the historian who would compile a Teniers catalog.

TENIERS'S STUDENTS

The logical place to begin a study of Teniers's influence is with his students. But, here one is confronted by the surprising fact that the art of Teniers's students is entirely unknown. The *Liggeren* of the Antwerp guild lists three students who all studied with David the Younger in the 1640s. There were no others.

The students listed in the *Liggeren* were Matheus Milese (apprenticed in 1640-1641), Gilles van Bolder (1643-1644), and Jan de Froey (1647-1648).[1] The records are almost entirely silent as to the careers of these men. Matheus Milese never became a master in Antwerp. The *Liggeren* notes him only as an apprentice. He probably did not long follow an artistic career. Gilles van Bolder became a master in 1645-1646, and in addition joined the Violieren Chamber of Rhetoric at about this same time. The *Liggeren* records that he left the Chamber of Rhetoric in 1645.[2] Jan de Froey also became a master in the Antwerp guild in 1652-1653.[3]

One naturally wonders about Teniers's three students. Were they all the remarkable failures that the records seem to indicate? We know of no works by Jan de Froey and van Bolder. If Milese became a master elsewhere there is no trace of his work either. Of course, if he abandoned art there would be no signed examples. Perhaps because David the Younger was so busy with his own growing career at the time he took these students he was a poor teacher. It may be that some of the poor-quality seventeenth-century copies of his paintings are the works of these students. In the absence of records and signatures there is no way of discerning what quality of work they did. The mysterious nature of Teniers's students is likely to remain so unless they eventually emerge from obscurity. At this point it is certain that they did not have any success as artists.

If David the Younger was a failure as a teacher, which he seems to have been, he did have an appreciable influence on the several members of his family who were also artists. Already noted is the difficult problem presented by the paintings of David the Elder that are executed in the style of his son.[4] David the Younger's brothers—Theodore (1619-1697), Julien II (1616-1679?), and Abraham (1629-1676?)—were artists. So was David the Younger's son, David III (1638-1685).

Among the brothers, Theodore is the least known. He entered the Antwerp guild in 1635-1636 as a wynmeester and student of David the Elder. We know of no works by Theodore, who seems to have engaged in dealing in art rather than in painting.[5] If he did paint, one might presume that his paintings would have reflected the style of David the Younger.

Julien II entered the guild at the same time as Theodore.[6] His style is known from a few works only, but these are quite similar to the paintings of David the Younger. For example, a signed *Interior with a Woman Peeling Apples*, Plate 37, is a very close copy of David the Younger's painting in the Fitzwilliam Museum, Cambridge. Julien's brushwork and draftsmanship are crude and heavy in comparison to those of his brother. Julien II produced gallery paintings and singeries in the manner of David the Younger. He also painted peasant genres, such as the 1662 *Village Fair*.[7] What little we do know of his style reveals that he was primarily an imitator of David the Younger. Julien II seems to have had little of any original personal style.

The best known of Teniers's brothers was Abraham. He entered the guild in 1645-1646 when David the Younger was dean.[8] While Abraham entered as a student of David the Elder, there is nothing about Abraham's style that reflects that of his father. Indeed, Abraham also imitated David the Younger. He is well known for his singeries, such as those in Madrid and Brussels. He also executed peasant genres. Abraham played a role in the reproduction of David the Younger's paintings as prints and it was he who published the first edition of the *Theatrum Pictorum* in 1658.

COLLABORATIVE WORKS

Despite the fact that David the Younger produced several thousand paintings in his long career, there are very few instances of his collaborating with other artists. With almost no exceptions David the Younger was called in to provide staffage and other genre elements in the paintings of those few artists with whom he did collaborate. The series of the *Nineteen Martyrs of Gorcum* is a notable exception in that Teniers himself must have begun these works and then summoned Gautier Guysaerts to finish them. This would seem to have been the logical course of events since the paintings were probably commissioned by David the Younger's son, Antoine. Most of the known cases of collaborations between David the Younger and other artists date from his mature period, although some occurred rather early in this period. At least one painting was created during 1643, at the height of David the Younger's early-mature period.

The series of paintings of Tasso's *Gerusalemme Liberata* (on which David the Younger collaborated with his father) may be included in the category of collaborations, yet it must remain separate in that these were works created before David the Younger had become a master.[9] There can be no doubt that both men worked on this series. But, perhaps it is best to view these paintings as a sort of training exercise for the youthful Teniers. Other such paintings eventually may be isolated in which David the Younger was "learning his lessons," so to speak.

The earliest example of a collaborative work (with the exception of the Tasso series) is the *Kitchen Interior*, Plate 5, on which David the Younger collaborated with Jan Davidsz de Heem. The painting bears Teniers's monogram and is dated 1643. Most of this panel is the work of David the Younger, and the style is typically that of his early-mature period. It is a combination of darker and cruder elements with some use of light colors and some areas of good draftsmanship. The composition is not quite as sophisticated as those of mature-period Teniers paintings, but it is acceptable and governed by diagonals. De Heem painted the grapes, which appear on the table at the center, and possibly some elements in the still life in the foreground. While there are areas of restoration, there is certainly no problem in identifying this as a Teniers work. In fact the steward in the kitchen may be a self-portrait.

There is one other painting in which Teniers collaborated with de Heem, as well as C. and P. de Vos and Gerard Seghers. This is a *Virgin and Child* in Vienna. A description is found in M. L. Hairs, *Les peintres flamands de fleurs aux XVIIe siècle,* on page 387.

David the Younger collaborated in a few instances with the landscapist, Jacques d'Arthois.[10] One of their finest productions is the *Landscape with Woodcutters* in Brussels, Plate 38. In this painting Teniers executed the staffage while the landscape is entirely by d'Arthois. Unlike the *Kitchen Interior*, in which David the Younger played a dominant role, the *Landscape with Woodcutters* illustrates well his abilities as a collaborator. His figures are quite harmonious with the landscape. In no sense do they overwhelm d'Arthois's style; they remain at once uniquely Teniers's and yet comfortable in their surrounding. Perhaps David the Younger learned the technique of successful collaboration from his father who frequently engaged in painting staffage for others. The *Landscape with Woodcutters* also illustrates David the Younger's debt to d'Arthois in the area of landscape. D'Arthois's handling of trees and foliage as well as his treatment of skies had an impact on David the Younger's treatment of similar elements in his own mature landscapes.

While it is obvious that David the Younger was influenced by the landscape style of Jacques d'Arthois, a more formidable influence came from the paintings of another master with whom he collaborated. David collaborated with Lucas van Uden on more occasions than he did with d'Arthois. One wonders whether this relationship might not have been encouraged by Teniers's obvious respect for van Uden's landscapes. Again, as with the paintings of d'Arthois, David the Younger easily combined his staffage with van Uden's backgrounds. Another painting from the Musées des Beaux-Arts Anciens in Brussels serves as a good example of the collaborations between those two artists. *Le Départ pour le Marché*, Plate 39, contains figures and some other elements by David the Younger in a typical van Uden landscape. The work probably dates from the first years of David the Younger's mature period, although it was most likely painted after 1643. The draftsmanship seems more competent and the colors lighter than those of the *Kitchen Interior*, for example. Teniers also painted the peasants's market cart and probably the small cottage in the left foreground. Van Uden's landscape elements, especially his skies and trees, are much like those Teniers did during this time. David the Younger also developed his outdoor lighting at least in part from the example of van Uden.

Later in his mature period David the Younger would use a more personal and highly refined landscape style than he did in the 1640s and early 1650s. But during these years his landscapes are quite like those of his two landscape collaborators. Their contributions to his style are clear and certain. In this case David the Younger's collaborations proved to be much more than mere business arrangements.

Teniers collaborated on many occasions with Jan van Kessel, a flower specialist. One of these works is a small *Temptations of St. Anthony in a Flower Garland*, Plate 40, again from Brussels. In this painting David the Younger executed a vignette of St. Anthony in a grotto in the center of van

Kessel's flowers. This little painting is undated, but must come from the 1650s on the basis of style. Van Kessel was almost a relative in that his mother was Paschasia Brueghel, sister of Jan Brueghel I. Jan van Kessel himself married the daughter of Ferdinand van Apshoven, one of Teniers's imitators. David the Younger must have known Jan van Kessel all his life and it was entirely logical that they would have collaborated frequently. David may have collaborated more often with van Kessel than with any other master. We know, for example, that the two worked on a series of at least nine paintings that were later reproduced as tapestries. These were the Moncada tapestries woven in the 1660s.[11] One example of the cartoons for these tapesteries has appeared recently in the art trade. This is the *Surrendering of the Keys to Count Moncada y Aragon*.[12] The work, dated 1664, was executed on copper. While it is not an especially attractive work, it is significant as one of a relatively small number of Teniers's paintings that may be accurately dated in this decade. Van Kessel surrounded the scene with putti, flowers, and grotesque decorations. Obviously the artists were not greatly concerned with creating a piece of fine art. This was simply a cartoon for the weavers. Van Kessel, along with several other artists, took some part in the merchandising of this series of tapestries.[13]

David the Younger's last known collaborator was Gautier Guysaerts, another flower specialist. We have already noted the supposed series that these two executed in 1675 or 1676. Since only one of these panels is known to survive, one suspects that it might have been the only painting of the series to have actually been finished. If all nineteen had indeed been painted, then Guysaerts would have had the honor of collaborating more frequently with David the Younger than any other master.

One wonders why David the Younger did not collaborate more often than he did. Perhaps he was simply too busy to form associations with others, however brief. It would almost seem that he should have created many paintings with other artists, given the popularity of genres and of his own paintings. But the fact remains that there are only a few such paintings. It may be significant that many of them are the landscapes from his younger years. As he became more established, he may have no longer felt an economic or a psychological need to attach himself to others.[14]

FOLLOWERS OF DAVID THE YOUNGER

David the Younger's pleasant genres and interesting drolleries prompted a large number of seventeenth-century artists to imitate his style and iconography. Almost without exception, these men had their own personal styles. Some were even specialists in categories not usually used by David the Younger. Many were well established and successful in their own right, yet still they imitated David the Younger's paintings from time to time. Their interest in David the Younger was mostly a matter of attraction rather than of emulation for the purpose of changing their styles. That this attraction was economically motivated is obvious. David the Younger was tremendously successful and there is little wonder that so many artists imitated his works.

Perhaps some of the lesser masters who imitated him did hope to enhance their own abilities by studying his paintings. This is essentially a moot point. Certainly David the Younger's paintings would have had much to offer in the way of lessons for some of these men. But it is likely that most of his imitators were motivated by his success—a sucess they hoped would accrue to them as well.

David Ryckaert III (1616-1661) was one of the earliest masters to be influenced by the paintings of David the Younger. Ryckaert's career somewhat parallels that of Teniers in that he too was a member of a large artistic family. Trained by his father, David III entered the Antwerp guild as a wynmeester in 1636-1637. He was employed by Archduke Leopold Wilhelm and was elected dean of the guild in 1651-1652.[15]

Ryckaert's paintings are compared to those of Teniers and Adriaen Brouwer. He seems to have been influenced by both these men. There is, however, a distinct group of Ryckaert paintings that were obviously meant to resemble the paintings of David the Younger, while at the same time he continued to create works in his own personal style. Perhaps his association with Brouwer and Teniers was similar to David the Younger's own fascination with Brouwer.

Ryckaert executed quite a large number of paintings in categories frequently used by David the Yougner. For example, he painted several versions of the *Temptations of St. Anthony*, the *Alchemist*, and peasant genres. The *Alchemist*, Plate 41, from 1648 easily recalls David's many *Alchemists*. Besides these better known Teniersian themes, Ryckaert also created more unusual works in other categories used by Teniers as well. Among these are paintings like the *Soldiers Plundering a Village* (Vienna, Kunsthistorisches Museum). He even executed a *Prodigal Son* on one occasion.[16] At times he only copied portions of Teniers's works. A Ryckaert *Interior* closely resembles a portion of the Teniers-De Heem *Kitchen Interior*. This painting is in the Emile Wolf gallery, New York, Plate 42. Most of the artist's paintings after Teniers seem to come from his middle years. Ryckaert is an interesting case of an established artist who still felt compelled to imitate the works of his colleague even when he was able to market his own paintings successfully.

There are a few paintings by the Antwerp master, Corneille Mahu, in which he copied David the Younger's *Liberation of St. Peter* paintings.[17] Mahu (1613-1689) seems to have been influenced by David the Younger otherwise.

William van Herp (1614-1677) studied with Damian Wortelmans and briefly with Hans Biermans.[18] He entered the Guild of St. Luke in 1637-1638.[19] He is best known as a genrist, although at times his work was influenced by such high-baroque masters as Rubens and Jacob Jordaens.[29] There are a few van Herp works that are quite close to paintings by David the Younger. Among these are a *Soldiers Attacking a Farm* (Vienna, Harrach collection), from 1664, and a *Family Interior* (London, Koetser Gallery, 1973). Van Herp imitated the peasant stereotypes of David the Younger, yet he did not copy them slavishly with the result that his peasants are fairly easy to recognize. They seem to have much rounder faces than those of Teniers. Van Herp's brush technique is quite unlike that of David the Younger in that van Herp made use of rather heavy areas of color. He tried to imitate David the Younger's grey glazes, as the *Family Interior* shows, but he did not understand how to work in thin glazes so as to produce delicate nuances of line and color.

Jan van den Hecke (1620-?) became a master in 1642. He was the student of Abraham Hack. Van den Branden noted that van den Hecke painted works with a palette similar to that found in Teniers's paintings.[21] He is known to have painted several peasant kermises like those of David the Younger.

Thomas van Apshoven (1622-1665) was one of the few seventeenth-century masters whose style actually comes close to that of David the Younger. Van Apshoven entered the Antwerp guild in 1645-1646 when David the Younger was dean. He was a student of his father, Ferdinand I.[32] Van Apshoven is known for his paintings of guardrooms, alchemists, and perhaps some singeries.[23] His paintings are like those of van Herp in that they display a limited understanding of David the Younger's technique. Thomas produced paintings that remind one of Teniers at first glance, but they quickly deteriorate into studies of very flat areas of paint upon closer examination. He simply did not have the ability to work in fragile glazes. His stereotyped figures provide evidence of his attempts to paint in a Teniers style, but even these seem flat and heavily drawn when they are compared to figures by David the Younger. Unlike Ryckaert, van Apshoven actually tried to paint like David the Younger. He attempted to sublimate his personal style to that of Teniers, but he failed. Van Apshoven may possibly be responsible for a large number of seventeenth-century paintings that look much like Teniers, but are not quite good enough to be his. Thomas van Apshoven's brother, Ferdinand II (1630-1694) mainly worked as an art dealer, but also produced a few Teniers-style paintings.

Matheus van Hellemont (1623-1674) was David the Younger's neighbor in the Lange Nieuwstraat in Antwerp.[24] He also entered the guild in 1645-1646 as a wynmeester. Van Hellemont later moved to Brussels where he was recorded as a member of the guild shortly before his death in 1674.[25] He apparently died in debt, perhaps as the result of a rather unfortunate life as an alcoholic. Van Hellemont frequently copied the paintings of David the Younger, often imitating specific works. One such is his *Interior with a*

Flayed Ox (Stockholm, Museum Hallwyl) that is very similar to versions of the painting by David the Younger. Van Hellemont also painted peasant interiors (for example, the painting in Milan, Poldi Pezzoli Museum) and *Alchemists*. The *Alchemist* seems to have been his favorite Teniersian theme. Examples of his alchemical paintings include those in Copenhagen and Rotterdam.

While Lambert de Hondt (ca. 1625-1665) is not known primarily for his paintings in a Teniers style, but rather for his military scenes and landscapes, he did occasionally produce a painting in which he imitated David the Younger. One such is a *Merrymaking* (Surrey, Cider House Galleries, 1976), which depicts a peasant kermis. The setting is quite typical of David the Younger's village scenes and the peasants closely resemble Teniers's stereotypes. De Hondt did not try to follow David the Younger's palette with the result that the painting is too colorful.

Egidius or Gillis van Tilborch (1625-1678) imitated David the Younger's genres. He seems to have confined his study of Teniers's paintings to this category. Examples of his paintings of peasants include the *Peasant Wedding* (Dresden, Gemäldesgalerie Alte Meister) and *Peasants Outside an Inn* (Robinson and Fisher sale, London, 1936). His genres are by no means exacting copies of Teniers, but rather personal interpretations of Teniers's style.

David Teniers III (1638-1685) may be included among the followers of David the Younger although his connection with his father is indeed slight. While we cannot dispute that David III painted some genres and other categories typical of the Teniers clan, his main interest was in portraiture and religious subject matter. He tried to emulate Van Dyck rather than his father. One must note that David III would have been better off trying to adopt his father's style. His paintings display a bad late-baroque style. He had no understanding of the high baroque that he tried to copy.

Nicolas van Verendael (1640-1691) produced many singeries in the manner of David the Younger. He was also an Antwerp master who entered the guild there in 1656-1657.[26] Most of his singeries seem to date from the period 1659 to 1687. Examples of these paintings are found in Antwerp, Brussels, Glasgow, and Cologne. Van Verendael also specialized in painting flower pieces.

Jan Thomas van Kessel (1677-1741) was the nephew and student of Ferdinand van Kessel. He studied with his uncle and also possibly with Peter Ijkens.[27] He entered the Antwerp guild in 1704.[28] Van Kessel's paintings seem to have mostly been genre scenes, although he did paint a few *Alchemists* similar to those of David the Younger. An example of an *Alchemist* by this artist is in the Vaduz collection, Lichtenstein.

Baltasar van den Bossche (1681-1715) studied with Gerard Thomas and became a master in 1697. Most of his career was spent in France.[29] He is noteworthy for his *Alchemists* in the Teniers style.

Pieter Angilles (1683/85-1734) was one of the last artists born in the seventeenth century whose style was influenced by David the Younger. His figure types sometimes recall those of Teniers.[30]

While there were many eighteenth-century masters who approved of and perhaps imitated the style of Teniers, many of these were anonymous artists whose approval at times ran to forgery. Only a few artists are mentioned below as followers of David the Younger in this century. His impact was far greater in the world of the graphic arts after 1700 than it was in paintings.

Baltasar Beschey (1708-1776) studied with Peter Strick although he was probably also influenced by Baltasar van den Bossche, his godfather.[31] He painted peasant genres, *Five Senses*, and *Alchemists* in a style slightly influenced by David the Younger. An example of the *Alchemist* by this artist is owned by the Fischer Collection in Pittsburgh. Besides his genres Beschey also painted religious works and portraits. Watteau de Lille (1731-1798) painted rural scenes after David the Yonger and at least one *Temptations of St. Anthony,* dated 1781 (Doisteau sale, Paris, 1909). Leonard de France (1735-1805) painted *Witches' Sabbats* after David the Younger as late as 1773.

5 Teniers and the Graphic Arts

The paintings of David the Younger inspired an incredibly large outpouring of prints executed after him. It is virtually impossible to arrive at an exact count of these prints. The British Museum itself owns over five hundred. Printmakers have copied David the Younger's paintings since the seventeenth century, although the majority of the prints after Teniers seem to have been made during the eighteenth century. This is most interesting since we tend to think of that century as the one whose artists turned away from the baroque. Obviously the light, pleasant genres of David the Younger had something in common with the decorative nature of the rococo. There are also a large number of nineteenth-century prints after David the Younger, but we will forego a discussion of these for the sake of brevity.

Most of the prints executed after David the Younger's paintings seem to have been reproductions of genres, although there are a goodly number of prints of the *Temptations of St. Anthony, Alchemists,* and a few reproducing occult subjects. Thus, the prints provide us with a very adequate summary of the output of David the Younger. They seem to come from every period of Teniers's career and they certainly tell us much about his popularity in his own and later centuries.

As we did with David the Younger's painter-followers, we will not attempt to include every printmaker who reproduced a Teniers painting in the following discussion. Such a list would become exhausting as well as boring. A representative group of seventeenth-century and eighteenth-century printmakers are included. Many of these individuals were also successful painters. This is especially true with some of the artists who reproduced David the Younger's copies for the *Theatrum Pictorum*. For a few of these artists, this was their only association with paintings by David the Younger. They are, however, the exceptions. Most graphic artists reproduced several of David the Younger's works. The large number of seventeenth-century prints after Teniers is most interesting because these works easily show us that David the Younger was indeed quite popular. They provide us with the reason for the great number of rather hastily executed Teniers paintings.

David the Younger himself produced a few etchings (there are approximately ten) that are identifiable as his own works. These are prints of genre scenes. He seems not to have worked very much in this medium. The British Museum owns this set as well as one mezzotint given to Teniers. There are also a number of other prints mentioned by Dutuit that he attributed to David the Younger.[1] Among these are a *Temptations of St. Anthony* (Dutuit, No. 11) and a series of the *Five Senses* (Nos. 15-19). These last are a group of allegorical peasant figures similar to paintings of this topic by David the Younger. Apparently David the Younger did not find much satisfaction in printmaking. Or, perhaps he simply did not have enough time to engage in this medium.

The artists who produced the engravings for the *Theatrum Pictorum* were Lucas Vostermann or Vorstermann (1595-1675), Jan van Troyen (active 1650-1690), Coryn Boel (1620-1668), Jan van Ossenbeeck (1624-1674), Pieter van Liselbetten or Lisebetius (1630-1678), Nicolas van Hoy (1631-1679), Coenrads Lauwers (1632?-1685), Jan van Popels (active in 1630-1640), Alexander Goubau (master in 1636), D. Claessens (perhaps the painter, Dominicus Claessens), and Ferdinand van Kessel II (1648-1696). Of these men several also reproduced other paintings by David the Younger. We will give them further mention in our discussion.

Abraham Teniers published the first edition of the *Theatrum Pictorum*. He is also known to have created a few prints after his brother's works. An example is the *Village Fete* (Dutuit, No. 1), Plate 43. Most of his interest in David the Younger's works seems to have been confined to the creating of imitative paintings rather than prints.

Jan van Troyen executed a large number of prints for the *Theatrum Pictorum* (some fifty-eight). Besides these, he also created portrait engravings of Don Juan of Austria after the painting by David the Younger. Van Troyen was much in demand as a reproductive engraver, counting Rubens among his clientele.

Coryn Boel worked on the *Theatrum Pictorum*, and he also created quite a few prints after David the Younger's paintings. He seems to have been interested in Teniers's paintings of genre. His themes include village surgeons, water doctors, and a print of an *Old Man Weighing Gold*. Like van Troyen, Boel was also well known as a reproductive engraver.

Wallerant Vaillant (1632-1677) was active in France and the Northern Netherlands. He worked in intaglio and mezzotints. His engravings after David the Younger are represented in the collections of the British Museum.

Frans van den Steen (1604-1672) was born in Antwerp, but was also active in Vienna where he worked for the royal household. Among his engravings of David the Younger's paintings was the *Covetous Man* (collection, Comte de Vence, 1761).

Sicrach Willemsens (1626-?) was a master in Antwerp in 1651. He is known to have reproduced one *Temptations of St. Anthony* after Teniers.

Pieter van Lisebetten engraved genres after David the Younger and reproduced his portrait of the Prince de Condé. He also engraved Pieter van Mol's portrait of David the Younger.

Besides his work on the engravings of the *Theatrum Pictorum,* Goubau also engraved Teniers's genres. He became a master in 1636-1637 and was active in Paris in 1655.

Ferdinand van Kessel seems to have specialized in the reproducing of David the Younger's singeries and other satirical animal paintings. Among his prints are *Cats in a Beer Hall* (Vienna, Kunsthistorisches Museum). His prints are also found in the collections at Besançon and Dresden.

Jacob Coelmans (1654-1735) engraved after Rubens and Teniers. His genres after David the Younger are represented by an example in the British Museum.

The Tardieus were a large family of French seventeenth- and eighteenth-century engravers. The Tardieu most often associated with David the Younger is Nicolas Henri (1674-1749) who engraved Teniers's paintings in the Crozat collection and the collection of the Comte de Vence. Two paintings that he engraved in the Vence collection were the *Alchemist* (Smith, No. 78) and *Le Déjeuner Flamand* (Smith, No. 79).

It is more likely that other members of the Tardieu family also made prints after Teniers in the eighteenth century. Isolating which artist created which print is complicated by the family tendency to sign works, "Tardieu."

Frans van den Wyngaerde was born in Antwerp in 1679. He etched genre paintings by David the Younger. Among his etchings are Dutuit, Nos. 33 and 34, *Dancing Peasants* and a *Village Scene,* respectively. This set of prints as well as others by him are owned by the British Museum.

Bernard Lepicié (1698-1755) was both writer and engraver. He is known to have created a print in 1747 of David the Younger's *Two Men Playing Cards in the Kichen of an Inn* (London, National Gallery, No. 2600).

The Viennese engraver, Andrew Altomonte (1699-1780) was connected with the family von Schwartzenberg. Perhaps this patronage accounts for his familiarity with works by Teniers. The British Museum owns a print by him after David the Younger's *Sacrifice of Abraham.*[2]

Le Bas (1701-1783), the famous French graphic artist, often turned to David the Younger for inspiration. Not only did he create a great many prints after Teniers, he also recommended David the Younger's works as objects of study for his many students. There is in a sense an entire group of French eighteenth-century prints after Teniers that come from the stimulus of Le Bas. Certainly Le Bas and his students found ready markets for these prints, just as did the family Tardieu. Le Bas's engravings of David the Younger's paintings were not confined to any specific category. Rather, they cover the entire range of his works. For example, Le Bas engraved the *Fisherman* (Smith, No. 82) in the Vence collection in 1750. He also reproduced the Louvre painting of the *Seven Acts of Mercy*, and *Achilles Recognized by Ulysses* (Smith, No. 52), the Louvre *Prodigal Son*, and a rare 1670 painting of *Adam and Eve* (Smith, No. 134).[3] Le Bas is believed to have created about one hundred prints after David the Younger.[4]

André Laurent was a student of Le Bas. He was the English engraver Andrew Lawrence (1708-1747) who made prints after David the Younger.

Thomas Major (1714?-1799) was a well known English reproductive engraver who frequently specialized in prints after Dutch and Flemish baroque masters. Among his prints after Teniers are the *Vocation of St. Peter* (Smith, No. 407) and a *Landscape with a Hunter* (Smith, No. 80).

Pierre Louis Surugue (1716-1772), a Parisian printmaker, reproduced David the Younger's allegorical figures of the *Four Seasons* (for example, London National Gallery, Nos. 857 and 858).

Noel le Mire (1724-1801) was a student of Jan Baptiste Descamps (Teniers's biographer) and of Le Bas. He frequently executed prints after David the Younger. The Portalis and Beraldi catalog of eighteenth-century prints lists fifty-seven.[5] One such is his engraving of *Latona Vengée* (Plate 44), in the Vence collection in 1750. The Fogg Museum owns a copy of this print. It reproduced David the Younger's *Latona and the Lycean Peasants* (Glasgow).

William Baillie (1723-1792), known as Captain Baillie, was an English engraver who at times turned to David the Younger for inspiration. His 1792 catalog included an *Alchymist* after Teniers, Plate 45.

Pierre François Basan (1723-1797) included David the Younger's paintings in several series of old-master reproductions from 1760, 1762, and 1779. He also engraved Teniers's paintings in both the Choiseul collection (1770) and the Vence collection. The Library of Congress owns a Basan engraving of a Teniers alchemist, titled *Le Grimoire d'Hypocrate*.[6]

Jacques Aliamet or Aliament (1726-1788) was another student of Le Bas. He reproduced Teniers's landscapes, an *Alchemist*, and the well-known *Arrival* and the *Depart for the Sabbat*. Aliamet may not have made many prints after David the Younger but these two scenes of witchcraft are quite important examples of Teniers's paintings of this type. Both paintings have disappeared and are known only from the prints of Aliamet.

Pierre Chenu (1730-1800?) may have been a student of Le Bas. He also engraved Teniers's paintings in the Vence collection, as well as many others.[7]

John Greenwood (1727-1792) was born in Boston in the American colonies and died in Margate, England. He was both a painter and engraver. He reproduced one Teniers painting of *Card Players*.

Richard Earlom (1742/43-1822), a London maker of reproduced and original prints executed a number of engravings after old-master paintings, including those of David the Younger. These are believed to date from between 1767 and 1770. Among his prints are the *Smokers* (from 1768) and *Le Mauvais Riche* (London, National Gallery, *Dives in Hell*).

The prints of Earlom bring this brief survey to a close with the beginning of the nineteenth century. The popularity of prints after David the Younger's paintings seems to have passed from Flanders to France by the end of the seventeenth century. This is probably due to a large number of print-makers in France during the eighteenth century rather than to a diminished respect for David the Younger in his homeland. Similarly, there were a great many prints after Teniers made in Germany in the nineteenth century.

That so many important graphic artists reproduced the paintings of David the Younger tells much about his position among the Flemish old masters. If his popularity fluctuated at times among the members of the public, he was not neglected by artists until modern times. Indeed he seems to have been far more popular in the artistic community than had been suspected.

As one might expect, prints after David the Younger vary considerably in quality and in their accuracy of reproduction. Some seem to have little about them to relate them to the original painting. Occasionally one encounters a print supposedly after Teniers that is nothing but a freehand copy of his works. Such prints are usually not successful. They tend to appear contrived and stiff.

Paintings by David the Elder were also reproduced by various printmakers so that one also encounters prints presumably after David the Younger that are actually copies of works by his father. These may frequently be prints from catalogs of collections.[8] Distinguishing between such prints may at times be difficult unless one is familiar with the particular painting in question.

The Teniers prints, like the Teniers tapestries, are a world in themselves. They are an obviously important tool in the compiling of a catalog. They also provide useful information on provenances and at times they are the only remaining records of lost or destroyed works.

Conclusion

There was a stylistic evolution in the career of David Teniers the Younger. We have observed this evolution to be most noticeable between 1632 and 1646. During these years David the Younger changed from a developing, hesitant young artist to an accomplished and popular master with his own distinctive mature style. David the Younger's popularity evolved almost as rapidly as his style did during these years. Gone were his periods of study and imitation. Teniers's association with Brouwer has been much overestimated. Certainly it was important, but the most important influence in his painting came from the Brueghel tradition. He was the best of the Brueghelians.

When we posit an early period in David the Younger's career we no longer have the problem of placing apparently inferior works into his oeuvre. We have simply recognized their right to exist. The early paintings are almost always of a lesser quality than those executed later on.

The existence of David the Younger's early-mature period is indisputable. It proves that there was also an early period in the artist's career. Obviously David the Younger became a better painter as he went along. We can observe the changes from painting to painting in the early-mature period to 1646. The dark heavy colors and weak diagonals disappear. So do the weak compositions and the hesitant draftsmanship. While David the Younger's painting technique improved, his brushstroke remained essentially the same. There is no problem in identifying his brushstroke in any period of his career. This is most helpful to us as a means of distinguishing authentic works.

Because David the Younger worked so rapidly and created so many paintings we are faced with the fact that there are bad paintings from his mature period. These we cannot ignore out of existence, but they should not hamper our connoisseurship. All one need do is look for that remarkably uniform brushstroke. If one finds it in a painting, one has a Teniers no matter how poor the quality seems. Quality need not be an absolute criterion for connoisseurship in the artist's mature period.

While it is not at all difficult to distinguish David the Younger's paintings from those of his followers, it is often much harder to distinguish their paintings one from the other. Here perhaps is our most problematic area in the study of Teniers.

We have found that David the Younger's obscurity is of a relative nature. He is seen today as a painter of quaint, frequently inferior, and always repetitive works. But modern scholars and many critics have tended to overlook David the Younger's important position in his own time. He was the artist who assumed dominance at the Brussels Court after the death of Rubens. In fact David the Younger's paintings became quite popular during the lifetime of Rubens. Was it not natural therefore that his star should rise with the death of the old master?

How much of David the Younger's popularity we must attribute to Archduke Leopold Wilhelm we may never know. But one suspects that Leopold Wilhelm was not the maker of David the Younger's fame. After all, Teniers had already established a widespread, even international, reputation when he entered the service of the archduke. And he continued his own very lucrative private business while in the archduke's employ.

If we are not content with David the Younger's importance in Flanders, if this does not prove he was a successful artist, then we need only look at his impact on other artists to see that he was indeed a significant master. The very fact that he was so frequently imitated proves that he was a success. Further, his great impact on the printmakers shows us that his contribution to art has been a lasting one.

David the Younger was not a bad painter, but a busy one. His very popularity occasioned the production of his many inferior works. We must always ignore these in favor of his best efforts. To these high-quality paintings we must add the remarkable nature of his influence on seventeenth- and eighteenth-century art. Then we will have the measure of this man as an artist.

The Plates

PLATE 1. David Teniers the Younger, *Saint Anthony in a Landscape*, about 1663 (Frankfurt, Staedelsches Kunstinstitut). Photo: Kurt Hasse, Frankfurt.

PLATE 2. David Teniers the Younger, *Still Life*, 1635 (Brussels, Musées Royaux des Beaux-Arts Anciens). Photo: copyright ACL.

PLATE 3. David Teniers the Younger, *The Seven Acts of Mercy*, 1660s (Paris, Louvre). Photo: Cliché des musées nationaux, Paris.

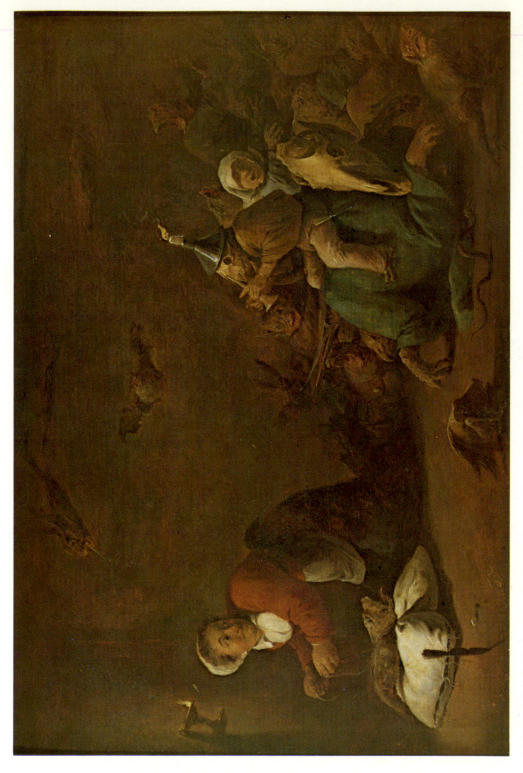

PLATE 4. David Teniers the Younger, *The Witch*, mid-1630s (Munich, Schleissheim Gallery). Photo: Bayerische Staatsgemaldesammlungen.

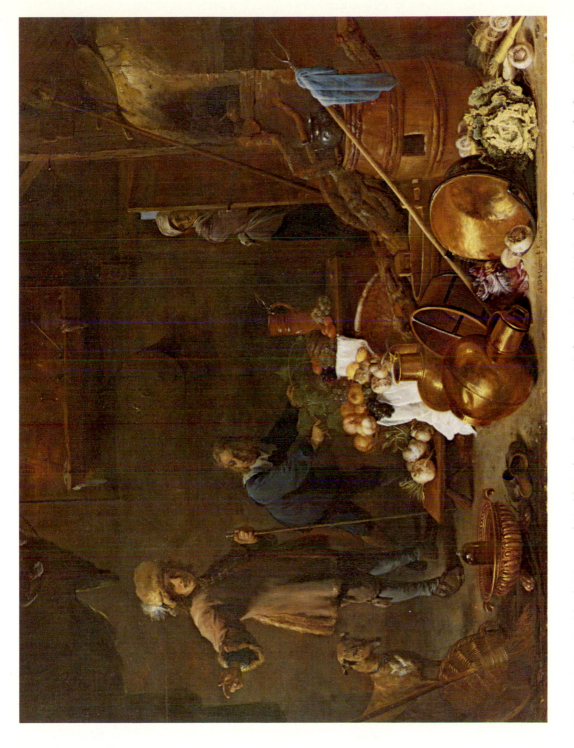

PLATE 5. Jan Davidsz de Heem and David Teniers the Younger, *Kitchen Interior*, 1643 (Los Angeles, Los Angeles County Museum of Art). Gift of H. F. Ahmanson & Co., in memory of Howard F. Ahmanson.

PLATE 6. David Teniers the Younger, *The Alchemist*, 1680 (Munich, Schleissheim Gallery).
Photo: Bayerische Staatsgemäldesammlungen.

PLATE 7. David Teniers the Younger, *Fat Kitchen*, 1643 (The Hague, Mauritshuis).

PLATE 8. David Teniers I and David Teniers the Younger, *Charles and Ubald Tempted by Nymphs,* from *Twelve Scenes from Tasso's Gerusalemme Liberata,* 1628 (Madrid, Prado, no. 1830).

PLATE 9. David Teniers I and David Teniers the Younger, *The Dream of Oradine*, from *Twelve Scenes from Tasso's Gerusalemme Liberata*, 1628 (Madrid, Prado, no. 1828).

PLATE 10. David Teniers I and David Teniers the Younger, *Charles and Ubald Searching for Rinaldo*, from *Twelve Scenes from Tasso's Gerusalemme Liberata*, 1628 (Madrid, Prado, no. 1827).

PLATE 11. David Teniers the Younger, *Christ on the Mount of Olives*, from the *Mysteries of the Rosary Series*, 1660s (Munich, Alte Pinakothek). Photo: Bayerische Staatsgemäldesammlungen.

PLATE 12. David Teniers the Younger, *The Nativity*, from the *Mysteries of the Rosary Series*, 1660s (Munich, Alte Pinakothek). Photo: Bayerische Staatsgemäldesammlungen.

PLATE 13. David Teniers the Younger, *The Card Players*, drawing, late 1630s (Vienna, Albertina). Photo: Lichtbildwerkstätte Alpenland.

PLATE 14. David Teniers the Younger, *Le Roi Boit* or *The Smoker*, late 1630s (Los Angeles, Los Angeles County Museum of Art, William Randolph Hearst Collection).

PLATE 15. David Teniers the Younger, *The Smoker*, 1643 (Munich, Alte Pinakothek). Photo: Bayerische Staatsgemäldesammlungen.

PLATE 16. David Teniers the Younger, *The Temptations of St. Anthony*, about 1650 (Madrid, Prado, no. 1822).

PLATE 17. David Teniers the Younger, *Landscape with Christ and the Pilgrims to Emmaus*, late 1640s (Los Angeles, Los Angeles County Museum of Art, William Randolph Hearst Collection).

PLATE 18. David Teniers the Younger, *Latona and the Lycian Peasants*, 1640s (Glasgow Art Gallery and Museum)

PLATE 19. Jan Brueghel I, *Latona and the Carien Peasants* (Frankfurt, Staedelsches Kunstinstitut). Photo: U. Edelmann, Frankfurt.

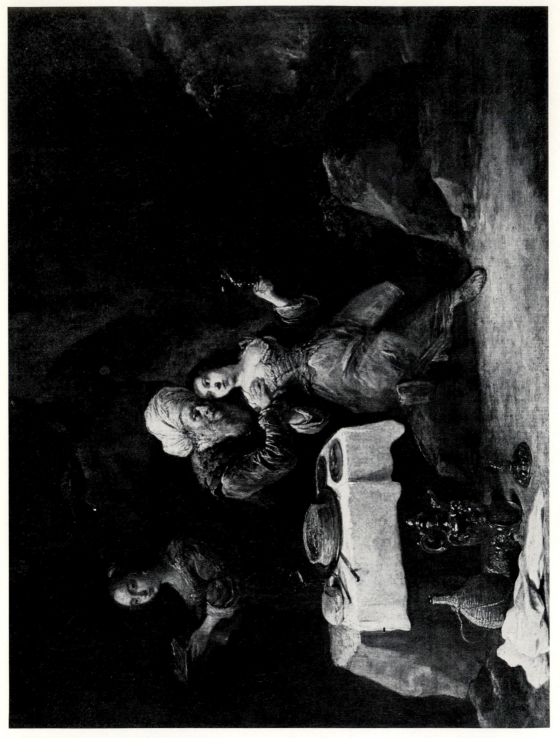

PLATE 20. David Teniers the Younger, *Lot and His Daughters*, mid-1630s (Munich, Alte Pinakothek). Photo: Bayerische Staatsgemäldesammlungen.

PLATE 21. David Teniers the Younger, *The Temptations of St. Anthony*, between 1638 to 1642 (Paris, Louvre).
Photo: Cliché des musées nationaux, Paris.

PLATE 22. David Teniers the Younger, *The Prodigal Son with the Prostitutes*, early 1640s (Munich, Alte Pinakothek). Photo: Bayerische Staatsgemäl-desammlungen.

94

PLATE 28. David Teniers the Younger, *The Temptations of St. Anthony*, mid-1640s (Antwerp, Museum Meyer van den Bergh). Photo: copyright ACL.

PLATE 24. David Teniers the Younger, *The Denial of St. Peter*, 1646 (Paris, Louvre). Photo: Cliché des musées nationaux, Paris.

PLATE 25. David Teniers the Younger, *The Alchemist*, mid- to late-1640s (Braunschweig, Herzog Anton Ulrich Museum). Photo: B. P. Keiser.

PLATE 26. David Teniers the Younger, *The Alchemist*, about 1650 (The Hague, Mauritshuis). Photo: A. Dingjan.

PLATE 27. David Teniers the Younger, *The Temptations of St. Anthony*, 1650s (Antwerp, Koninklijk Museum van Schoone Kunsten). Photo: copyright ACL.

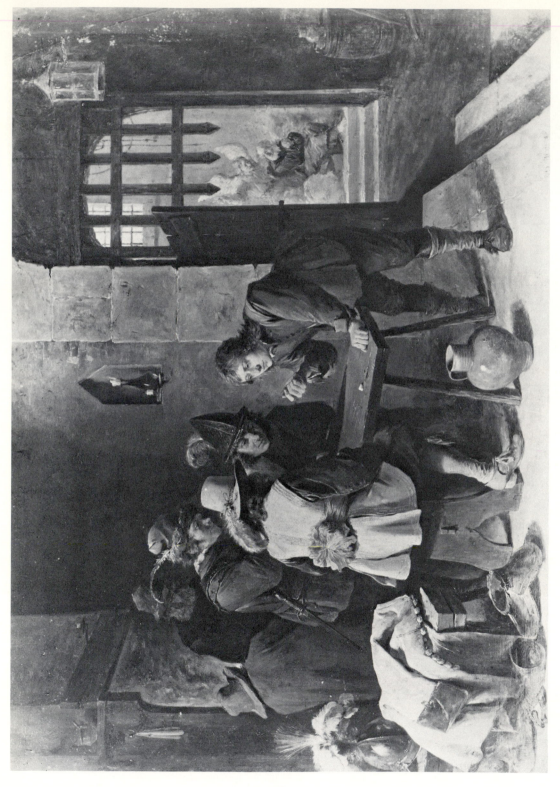

PLATE 28. David Teniers the Younger, *The Deliverance of St. Peter*, 1660s (London, Wallace Collection). **Photo:** reproduced by permission of the Trustees of the Wallace Collection.

100

PLATE 29. Aliamet, *The Alchemist,* engraving after Teniers, mid–eighteenth century. Photo: Rijksbureau voor Kunsthistorische documentatie.

PLATE 30. David Teniers the Younger, *The Alchemist*, 1640s (San Diego, Fine Arts Gallery).

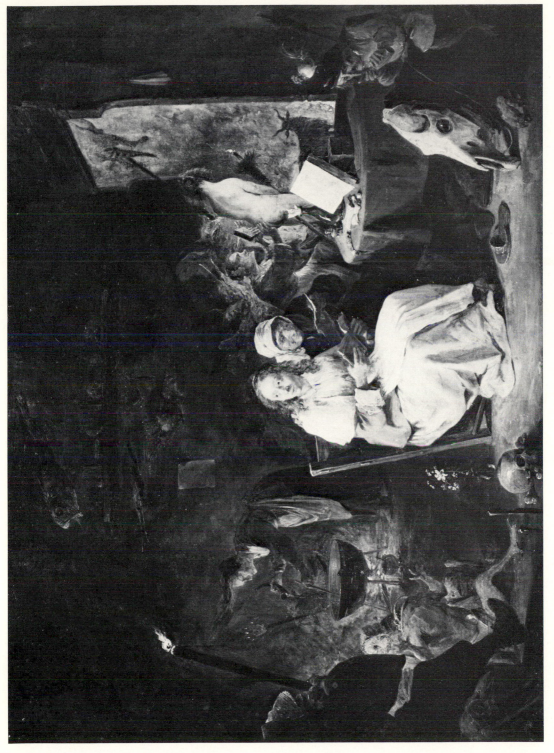

PLATE 31. David Teniers the Younger, *Incantation Scene*, early 1650s (New York, New York Historical Society). Photo: courtesy of the New York Historical Society.

PLATE 32. David Teniers the Younger, *The Good Samaritan*, after a painting by Bassano, late 1650s (New York, Metropolitan Museum of Art). Gift of Henry G. Marquand, 1889; Marquand Collection.

PLATE 33. David Teniers the Younger, *The Madonna of the Cherries*, after a painting by Titian, late 1650s (London, Wallace Collection). Photo: reproduced by permission of the Trustees of the Wallace Collection.

105

PLATE 34. Gautier Guysaerts and David Teniers the Younger, *Blessed Jan van Weert in a Flower Garland*, 1675 (Amsterdam, Rijksmuseum). Photo: copyright Fotocommissie Rijksmuseum.

PLATE 35. David Teniers the Younger, *The Alchemist*, late 1670s (Madrid, Prado).

107

PLATE 36. David Teniers the Younger, *The Assumption of the Virgin,* from the *Mysteries of the Rosary Series,* 1660s (Munich, Alte Pinakothek). Photo: Bayerische Staatsgemäldesammlungen.

PLATE 37. Julien Teniers II, *Interior with a Woman Peeling Apples* (Copenhagen, National Museum). Photo: H. Petersen.

PLATE 38. Jacques d'Arthois and David Teniers the Younger, *Landscape with Woodcutters*, early 1640s (Brussels, Musées Royaux des Beaux-Arts Anciens). Photo: copyright ACL.

PLATE 39. Lucas van Uden and David Teniers the Younger, *Le Départ pour le Marché*, about 1644 (Brussels, Musées Royaux des Beaux-Arts Anciens). Photo: copyright ACL.

PLATE 40. Jan van Kessel and David Teniers the Younger, *The Temptations of St. Anthony in a Flower Garland*, 1650s (Brussels, Musées Royaux des Beaux-Arts Anciens). Photo: copyright ACL.

PLATE 41. David Ryckaert III, *The Alchemist*, 1648 (Brussels, Musées Royaux des Beaux-Arts Anciens). Photo: copyright ACL.

PLATE 42. David Ryckaert III, *Kitchen Interior*, 1640s (New York, Emile Wolf Gallery). Photo: Eric Pollitzer.

PLATE 43. Abraham Teniers, *Village Fete*, engraving after David Teniers the Younger, probably 1650s (London, British Museum). Photo: reproduced by courtesy of the Trustees of the British Museum.

115

PLATE 44. Noel le Mire, *Latona Vengée*, engraving after David Teniers the Younger, before 1750 (Cambridge, Massachusetts; Harvard University Fogg Museum of Art). Photo: courtesy of the Fogg Art Museum. Bequest of the Francis Calley Gray Fund.

PLATE 45. William Baillie, *The Alchymist*, engraving after David Teniers the Younger, 1792. Photo: Rijksbureau voor Kunsthistorische Documentatie, The Hague.

117

PLATE 46. Peter Paul Rubens, *Emblem of Christ Appearing to Constantine*, sketch, 1621 to 1622 (Philadelphia, John G. Johnson Collection, Philadelphia Museum of Art).

PLATE 47. David Teniers I and David Teniers the Younger, *A Scene in Godfroy's Camp*, from *Twelve Scenes from Tasso's Gerusalemme Liberata*, 1628 (Madrid, Prado, no. 1826).

PLATE 48. David Teniers I and David Teniers the Younger, *Armida in Battle*, from *Twelve Scenes from Tasso's Gerusalemme Liberata*, 1628 (Madrid, Prado, no. 1835).

Notes

PREFACE

1. Adolf Rosenberg, *David Teniers der Jungere: Künstler Monographien* 8 (Leipzig and Bielefeld: Knackfuss, 1898).

2. Roger de Peyre, *David Teniers Biographie Critique* (Paris: Laurens, 1910).

3. Among the best of the modern studies were two produced by Hans Vlieghe dealing respectively with Teniers's activities for Leopold Wilhelm and with a survey of published documentation on David the Younger. See the bibliography for entries.

INTRODUCTION

1. Cornelis De Bie, *Het Gulden Cabinet van de edele vry schilderconst* (Antwerp: Myssens, 1661), pp. 334-39.

2. Roger de Piles, *Abrégé de la vie des peintres* (1669; reprint ed., Hildesheim: Olms, 1969), p. 432.

3. J. von Sandrart, *Teutsche Academie der Bau-Bild-und-Mahlerey Kunste* (1675; reprint ed., Munich: A. P. Peltzer, 1925), pp. 194, 231.

4. Arnold Houbraken, *De Groote Schouburgh der Nederlandsche Konst-schilders en Schilderessen* (1718-1721; reprint ed., Maastricht: Lieter-Uypels, 1943-1944, 1953), pp. 272-73.

5. Jean-Baptiste Descamps, *Vie des peintres flamands et hollandais* (1754; reprinted ed., Marseilles: Barle, 1842), vol. 3, pp. 5-15.

6. Max Doerner, *The Materials of the Artist and Their Use in Painting* (New York: Harcourt, Brace & Co., 1949), p. 355.

7. Antoine Joseph Dezailler d'Argenville, *Abrégé de la vie des plus fameux peintres* (1762; reprint ed., Geneva: Minkoff, 1972), vol. 3, pp. 387-91.

8. P. Mariette, *Abecedario* (Paris: J. B. Dumaulen, 1859-60), vol. 5, pp. 286-88.

9. J. Dewert, "Origine Wallonne des Peintres Teniers," *Bulletins de la commission royale d'histoire de Belgique* 80 (1911): 14.

10. Ibid.

11. Ibid., pp. 4-5, 14-15.

12. Ibid., pp. 7-8, 19-20, 25-26.

13. For Julian Joachimzoon see Franz Joseph Peter van den Branden, *Geschiedenis der Antwerpsche Schilderschool* (Antwerp: Buschmann, 1878-1883), p. 751. He has also been discussed by several other writers. The best survey of David Teniers the Elder is Erik Duverger and Hans Vlieghe, *David Teniers der Ältere* (Utrecht: Haentjens, Dekker, and Gumbert, 1971).

CHAPTER 1

1. Van den Branden, *Geschiedenis,* pp. 981-82.

2. Ibid., p. 982.

3. Philippe-Felix Rombouts and Theodore van Lerius, *De Liggeren en andere historische Archiven van het Antwerpsche St. Lucasgilde* (1864-1876; reprint ed., Amsterdam: N. Isracl, 1961), vol. 2, p. 35.

4. Erik Duverger, "Bronnen voor de geschiedenis van de artistiche betreffingen tussen Antwerpen en de voordelijke Nederlanden tussen 1632 en 1648," *Miscellanea Josef Duverger* (Gent: n.d. Vereniging voor de Geschiedenis der Textual kunsten, n.d.), vol. 1, p. 65.

5. Ibid.

6. J. Denucé, "Brieven en Documenten betreffende Jan Breughel I en II," *Bronnen voor de Geschiedenis van de Vlaamsche Kunst* 3 (1934): 98.

7. Ibid., p. 99

8. Svetlana Alpers, *The Decoration of the Torre de la Parada. Corpus Rubenianum* (Brussels: Arcade, 1971), vol. 9, pp. 42-43.

9. John Vermoelen, "Teniers le Jeune; sa vie, ses oeuvres," *Journal des Beaux Arts et de la Littérature* (December 15, 1864): 180. Vermoelen published the marriage certificate as it is found in the Stadsarchief, Antwerp.

10. Denuce, "Brieven en Documenten," pp. 100-12.

11. Ibid., p. 110. See also Protocollen Notaris J. le Rousseau 1628, f°86, Stadsarchief, Antwerp.

12. John Vermoelen, "Notes Historiques sur David Teniers et sa famille," *Revue historique, nobiliaire, et bibliographique* 8 (1870-1871): 158.

13. Van den Branden, *Geschiedenis,* p. 990.

14. Duverger, "Bronnen voor de geschiedenis," p. 355.

15. Denucé, "Brieven en Documenten," p. 129.

16. Vermoelen, "Notes Historiques," p. 156.

17. Rombouts and van Lerius, *De Liggeren,* vol. 2, pp. 153, 165.

18. Frans Mares, "Beiträge zur Kenntnis der Kunstbestregungen des Erzherzogs Leopold Wilhelm," *Jahrbuch der Kunsthistorischen Sammlungen der Allerhöchsten Kaiserhauses in Wien* 5 (1887): 345.

19. Mss. divers 1374, f°7, Archives générales du royaume, Brussels. This was published in *Archives Bibliothèques et Musées de Belgique* (1928): 77, by J. Lefevre, but is reproduced here since its existence is not well known.

20. W. Speth-Holterhoff, *Les peintres flamands de cabinets d'amateurs au XVIIe siècle* (Brussels: Elsevier, 1957), pp. 141-43.

21. David Teniers the Elder is known to have worked at times for the Brussels

court prior to the entry of Leopold Wilhelm. Perhaps David the Younger's means of entry was the good name of his father.

22. Hans Vlieghe, "David Teniers II en het hof van aartshertog Leopold Wilhelm en Don Juan van Oostenrijk, 1647-1659," *Gentse Bijdragen tot de Kunstgeschiedenis* 19 (1961-1966): 116.

23. Hans Schneider, "Een prinseleyke Opdracht aan David Teniers D. J.," *Nederlandse Oudheidkundige Jaarboek* series 4 2 (April 1933): 37.

24. David the Elder's paintings were to be found in the collections of such notables as Archdukes Albert and Isabella.

25. Van den Branden's account of the "lesson" given to David the Younger by Rubens hardly constitutes a case for including Rubens as one of Teniers's teachers.

26. This painting is reproduced in Duverger and Vlieghe, *David Teniers der Ältere*, plate 39.

27. These paintings go by the traditional title, *Fifteen Scenes from the Life of Mary*. They were painted for Anna-Maria Bonnarens, wife of David Teniers III. They were listed in an inventory of her collection in 1671, possibly indicating the date when they were painted as one from the 1660's. The paintings passed to the collection of Max Emmanuel of Bavaria in 1710 and thence to the Alte Pinakothek. See Oscar Schellekens, *Les Trois David Teniers Peintres* (Termonde: Grotjans-Willems, 1912), pp. 33-34.

28. For a discussion of David the Elder and Elsheimer, see Duverger and Vlieghe, *David Teniers der Ältere*, passim.

29. This painting was engraved by Cornelis Galle. It is illustrated in Duverger and Vlieghe, *David Teniers der Ältere*, plate 25, who also reproduce *The Shepherds's Visit*, plate 44.

30. David the Younger included a very similar figure in his *Interior of an Inn* (Amsterdam, Rijksmuseum).

31. Gerard Knuttel, *Adriaen Brouwer* (The Hague: L. J. C. Boucher, 1972), pp. 14-25.

32. Ibid., pp. 95-96.

33. I wish to thank my husband for his assistance in these experiments with pigments and glazes.

34. These paintings are included in a section on late Brouwer works in Knuttel, *Adriaen Brouwer*, pp. 14-25.

35. Georges Marlier, *Pierre Brueghel le Jeune* (Brussels: Robert Finck, 1969), pp. 121-22.

36. Ibid. Marlier recognized this many versions of the *Flemish Proverbs* as authentic works by Pieter II.

37. For a description and explanation of the proverbs see Ibid., passim.

38. Reproduced in Ibid., p. 430, fig. 279.

39. Some of these similarities were noted in G. von Terey, "David Teniers und der Samtbreughel," *Kunstchronik und Kunstmarkt* 47 (August 25, 1922): 780-87.

40. S. V. Grancsay, "Arms and Armor in Paintings by David Teniers the Younger," *Walters Art Gallery Journal* 9 (1946): 22-40.

41. American Art Association sale, 1937. The painting measured 21½ by 31 inches.

42. Francine Claire Legrand, *Les peintres flamands de genre au XVIIe siècle*

(Brussels: Meddens, 1963), p. 128.

43. Examples of peasant kermises in which nobility and bourgeoisie appear with peasants include Jan Brueghel I's *Village Fair* (Windsor Castle) and Lucas van Valkenborch's *Autumn* (Vienna, Kunsthistorisches Museum).

44. Jan Piet Ballageer, "Bij het 17de-eeuwse schilderij-fragment 'De Werken van Barmhartigheid' in de Koninklijke Musea voor Schone Kunsten van Belgie te Brussel," *Musées Royaux des Beaux-Arts Bulletin* (1969): 141-48.

45. Ibid., p. 143.

46. Ibid., pp. 142-43.

47. W. Speth-Holterhoff, *Les peintres flamands de cabinets d'amateurs au XVIIe siècle* (Brussels: Elsevier, 1957), p. 129.

48. David the Elder painted one *Kunstkamer* (Brussels, Girous, 1959) and the theme was explored by Jan Brueghel I's many paintings of the allegories of the five senses.

49. The figure resembles the peasant types of Pieter Brueghel II. The witch is actually adopted from the Flemish proverb of the spiteful woman that appears in many of the Brueghel paintings. The proverb, *"zij zou de duivel op een kussen binden,"* or "she could tie the devil on a cushion," seems to be a popular corruption of the legend of St. Margaret. There is a long tradition of associating the devil, tied to a pillow, with evil women. The idea appears frequently in Flemish literature and art in the seventeenth century. With it is usually found the association of St. Margaret's encounter with the devil. For example, Roemer Visscher wrote of St. Margaret in his *Brabbeling* (Amsterdam, 1614), *"De beste Griet seyt Mieuwers diemen vant, Was die de Duyvel op het cussen bant."* From Het seste Schock van de Quicken, p. 78. Tying the devil to a pillow also appeared in Pieter Brueghel I's *Dulle Griet,* where the reference is to evil or strong-willed women.

The notion of tying up the devil has continued in popular Flemish culture. Jan Grauls noted in his *Volkstaal en Volksleven in het werk van Pieter Brueghel* (Antwerp: Standard Bokhandel, 1957), p. 25, an inscription taken from a gravestone in Ghent dated 1838: *"Hier ligt begraven mijn booze Griet, Dat se in d'helle is, hoop ik niet, Dat se in den hemel is, geloof ik niet, Maer dat se in'tvaghevier wordt gheslaghen, Soo langh sy my op d'aerde hevet gheplaghen."* Grauls has carefully established the origins of this proverb of the devil with the legend of St. Margaret, and has traced them to the *Dulle Griet* and the *Proverbs* painting. See pp. 24-28 and 32-35. Dulle Griet, thus, is evil Griet or Margaret.

50. This painting is further discussed on page 57.

CHAPTER 2

1. Mss. divers 2631, Sanct Joan de 1651, f°300 verso. Archives générales du royaume, Brussels.

2. For a discussion of when David the Younger became the ayuda de camera, see Faith P. Dreher, "Discussion; David Teniers II Again," *Art Bulletin* 59 (March 1977): 108-11.

3. A. Wauters, "David Teniers et son fils, le troisième du nom," *Société royale d'archéologie de Bruxelles, Annales* 2 (1897): 10-11.

4. Insolvente Boedelskamer; Familie Musson, f°512, Stadsarchief, Antwerp. In Hans Vlieghe, "David Teniers II en het hof van aartshertog Leopold Wilhelm en Don Juan van Oostenrijk, 1647-1659," *Gentse Bijdragen tot de Kunstgeschiedenis* 19 (1961-1966): 133.

5. Franz Mares, "Beiträge zur Kenntnis der Kunstbestregungen des Erzherzogs Leopold Wilhelm," *Jahrbuch der Kunsthistorischen Sammlungen der Allerhöchsten Kaiserhauses in Wien* 5 (1887): 349-50, 355.

6. Cornelis De Bie, Het Gulden Cabinet van de edele-vry Schilderconst (Antwerp: Myssens, 1662), p. 339; and A. de Witte, "La medaille honorifique offerte à David Teniers le Jeune par Leopold Guillaume, Archiduc d'Austriche Governeur des Pays Bas esp," *Annales du Cercle archéologique de la Ville et de l'ancien Pays de Termonde* (1903). Philip may also have presented Teniers with a medal. See Wauters, "David Teniers," p. 19.

7. M. De Maeyer, *Albrecht en Isabella en de Schilderkunst* (Brussels: Paleis der Academien, 1955), p. 267, and Item no. 50 in the documents wherein is reproduced the 1732 inventory of the royal collections taken after the fire. The document is conserved in the Archives générales du royaume, Brussels, Ouvrages de la Cour no. 399 reg. f° 172-176.

8. Van den Branden, *Geschiedenis, der Antwerpsche Schilderschool* (Antwerp: Buschmann, 1878-1883), p. 998. Van den Branden believed that Claire-Eugénie Teniers died in 1656. The child who died was actually Anne-Catherine as recorded in John Vermoelen, "Notes Historiques, sur David Teniers et sa famille," *Revue historique, nobiliare, et bibliographique* 8 (1870-1871): 157.

9. Van den Branden, *Geschiedenis*, p. 998.

10. This house was located near the precincts of the court in a neighborhood that was both prestigious and convenient. David the Younger had rented this house prior to buying it. See Wauters, "David Teniers," p. 11

11. Reg. Matr. sancti-Jacobi, 1645-1667, f°95 verso. Archives de la Ville de Bruxelles.

12. Van den Branden, *Geschiedenis*, p. 999.

13. Ibid., pp. 1002-3.

14. Ibid., pp. 100-1. See also Dreher, "Discussion," pp. 108-11.

15. John Vermoelen, "Notes Historiques," p. 146.

16. John Vermoelen, "Teniers le Jeune; sa vie ses oeuvres," *Journal des Beaux Arts et de la Littérature* (January 31, 1865): 10.

17. John Vermoelen, "Notes Historiques," p. 146.

18. Dreher, "Discussion," pp. 108-11.

19. John Vermoelen, "Notes Historiques," and other authors. This document is written in such poor French that it is difficult to decide whether it actually means that David the Younger was granted his patent of nobility by Philip IV. This author cannot agree with Dreher that this document proves absolutely that it was Philip IV who granted the letter patent.

20. De Bie, *Het Gulden Cabinet*, p. 339.

21. J. von Sandrart, *Teutsche Academie der Bau-Bild-und-Mahlerey Kunste* (1675; reprint ed., Munich: A. P. Peltzer, 1925), pp. 194, 231.

22. Mares, "Beiträge zur Kenntnis," p. 355.

23. *Serenissimo Principi Leopoldi Guilielmo, Archiduci, Austriae, etc. Domino*

suo clementissimo hoc amphitheatrum picturarum ex suae serenit arche-typis delineatum sua manu dedicacit. Anno MDCLVII. David Teniers suae Ser. pictor domesticus. Men vint dees printboecken te coop t'Antwerpen by Abraham Teniers.

24. Some of these little paintings seem to have stayed in the possession of the Teniers family. See Napoléon de Pauw, "Les trois peintres David Teniers et leurs homonymes," *Academie royale d'archéologie de Belgique*, Annales serie 5, 50 (1889): 351-52.

25. All versions of the 1660 edition bear the same title as the *Schilder-Thooneel*. In 1673 the second edition was printed again and offered for sale by the widow of Abraham Teniers. For a note on this edition see Max Rooses, *Geschiedenis der Antwerpsche Schilderschool* (Gent: Hoste, 1879), p. 588.

26. *Theatrum Pictorum David Teniers*, Antwerp: H. & C. Verdussen, 1684.

27. Konstantin Simillion, "Levensschets van David Teniers den jonge," *De Vlaamsche School* 10 (1864): 40-41.

28. Ibid., pp. 41-43.

29. Vermoelen, "David Teniers le Jeune," p. 188.

30. Simillion, "Levensschets," p. 41.

31. Charter p417², Stadsarchief, Antwerp.

32. Simillion, "Levensschets," p. 47.

33. The Marquis of Caracena was godfather by proxy to Louis Teniers, born in 1662. Registr Baptisterii Parochialiis Ecclesiae sancti-Jacobi Montis frigidi 1653-1667, f ° 233. Archives de la Ville de Bruxelles.

34. The design of this painting reminds one somewhat of paintings by David Teniers the Elder, although there can be absolutely no doubt that it is a work by David the Younger.

35. Kieffer sale, Paris, 1969: Gallery Georges Petit, 1922.

36. Formerly collection Bart. Kessingen, Spik, 1955.

37. Louis Reau, *Iconographie de l'art chretien* (Paris: Presses Universitaires de France, 1958), vol. 3, p. 105. See also Erik Larsen, "Les Tentations de St. Antonine de Jerome Bosch," *Revue Belge d'archeologie et d'histoire de l'art* 19 (1950): 9-10.

38. Herbert Thurston and Donald Attwater, eds. *Butler's Lives of the Saints* (New York: P. J. Kennedy & Sons, 1956), vol. 6, p. 105.

39. Ibid., pp. 106-7.

40. Ibid.

41. Demons in monk's habits are found in the paintings of Bosch where they were probably meant to personify heretics. For a discusion of this see Charles D. Cuttler, "Witchcraft in a Work by Bosch," *Art Quarterly* (Summer, 1957): 131.

42. Thurston and Attwater, *Butler's Lives of the Saints,* p. 107.

43. St. Athanasius's life of Anthony is reproduced in Phillip Schaff and Henry Wace, eds., *The Nicene and Post-Nicene Fathers of the Christian Church*, 2nd series (Grand Rapids: 1953), vol. 4, pp. 188-221.

44. Charles D. Cuttler, "The Temptations of St. Anthony in Art from Earliest Times to the First Quarter of the XVI Century." (Ph.D. diss., New York University, 1951), passim.

45. St. Jerome's account may be found in J. P. Migne, ed., *Patrologiae Latinae* (Paris: Garnier, 1883), vol. 23, pp. 17-29.

46. Ryan Granger and Helmut Ripperger, trans., *The Golden Legend of Jacobus de Varagine* (London: Longmans Green & Co., 1941), Part 1, pp. 99-102.

47. Cuttler, "The Temptation," pp. 5-6.

48. Réau, *Iconographie de l'art chrétien,"* pp. 104-5. See also Larsen, "Les Tentations de St. Antoine," pp. 9-10. The fire is a reference to the disease known as St. Anthony's fire, probably a form of ergotism, which was treated by the medieval Hospital Order of St. Anthony. The saint may also have assumed some role as a patron-protector against fires, according to Larsen.

49. Réau, *Iconographie de l'art chrétien,"* pp. 1051-52.

50. Schaff and Wace, eds., *The Nicene and Post-Nicene Fathers*, p. 198.

51. They somewhat resemble the eggs with legs found in the Brueghel paintings, although the symbolism is quite different in the Teniers paintings.

52. Alfred de Lostalot, "Collection de M. J. de Lessingen," *Gazette des Beaux Arts* 8 (1876): 483-93.

53. J. A. van de Graaf, *Het De Mayerne Manuscript* (Mijdrecht, 1958), #23, f°6 of Sloan Mss. 2052, British Museum.

54. E. E. Ploss et al., *Alchemia Ideologie und Technologie* (München: Moos, 1970), p. 122.

55. Kurt K. Doeber, *The Goldmakers* (Westport, Conn.: Greenwood, 1972), lists several hundred titles published between 1600 and 1700.

56. Lynn Thorndike, *A History of Magic and Experimental Science* (New York, 1958), vol. 7, p. 163.

57. Ibid., pp. 197-201.

58. Émile Grillot de Givry, *Witchcraft, Magic, and Alchemy*, trans. J. Courtenay Locke (1928; reprint ed., New York: Bonanza, n.d.), pp. 375-78.

59. Ibid., pp. 377-78.

60. Examples of such paintings may be found in the Prado.

61. Jacob Rosenberg, "On the Meaning of a Bosch Drawing," in Millard Meiss, ed., *De Artibus opuscula XL—Essays in Honor of Erwin Panofsky* (New York: New York University Press, 1961), pp. 422-23.

62. For a discussion of several Dutch proverbs concerning negative attributes of the owl see C. Kruijskamy, *Groot Woordenboek der Nederlandse Taal* (s'Gravenhage, 1961), p. 2116.

63. Seymour Slive, *Frans Hals* (London: Phaidon, 1970), pp. 151-52. Slive quoted this proverb in reference to the owl as a symbol of evil and folly in Hals's *Malle Babbe*.

64. Rosenberg, "On the Meaning of a Bosch Drawing," pp. 423-26.

65. Slive, *Frans Hals*, pp. 151-52.

66. John Read, *The Alchemist in Life, Literature, and Art* (London: Nelson & Sons, 1947), p. 79.

67. Only two other instances are known in which David the Younger used this motif.

68. Eduard de Moreau, *Histoire de l'église en Belgique* (Bruxelles, l'Edition Universelle, 1952), vol. 5, pp. 368-69.

69. Ibid., p. 370.

70. Ibid., p. 361.

71. Ibid., p. 369.

72. Ibid., pp. 367-68. The *Disquisitionum magicarum* of the Jesuit Martin del Rio (born in Antwerp, 1551 and died in Louvain, 1608) was typical of such witchcraft manuals. It appeared in 1593 and contained descriptions of witches' activities as well as advice on how to conduct inquisitions. One of the most influential seventeenth-century treatises on witches was Fra Francesco Maria Guazzo's *Compendium Maleficarum*, published in Milan in 1610 and in a second edition in 1626. This work is still considered an authoritative source for seventeenth-century ideas about witches and is well known for its illustrations of the sabbat. The similarities in the descriptions of witchcraft published in these two books reflect a uniformity of ideas about witches found throughout Europe in the century.

73. Wade Baksin, *A Dictionary of Satanism* (New York: Philosophical Library, 1972), p. 136.

74. Ibid., pp. 138-39.

75. The food served at a sabbat consisted of corpses, preferably stolen from gibbets or exhumed, the bodies of unbaptised infants, and other such unpalatable substances.

76. Margaret Alice Murray, *The Witch-Cult in Western Europe* (Oxford: Clarendon Press, 1921), p. 150.

77. H. E. Wedeck, *Treasury of Witchcraft* (New York: Philosophical Library, 1961), p. 157.

78. Charles D. Cuttler, "Witchcraft in a Work by Bosch," *Art Quarterly* 20 (1957): 132-38.

79. Murray, *The Witch-Cult*, pp. 279-80.

80. Ibid., p. 146.

81. Ibid., p. 49.

82. Biaget, *Examen of Witches*, trans. E. A. Ashwin (1609; reprint ed., London: Hooker, 1929), p. 42.

CHAPTER 3

1. The letter to Leopold is reproduced in Konstantin Simillion, "Levensschets van David Teniers den jonge," *De Vlaamsche School* 10 (1864): 83. The second letter to David III was published by John Vermoelen, "Teniers le Jeune; sa vie, ses oeuvres," *Journal des Beaux Arts et de la Littérature* (January 31, 1865): 37.

2. Vermoelen, "Teniers le Jeune," pp. 36-37.

3. Ibid., p. 37.

4. We know that David the Younger attempted various public sales from time to time in order to raise money. One such was held in 1666, another in 1683. See A. Wauters, "David Teniers et son fils, le troisième du nom," *Société royale d'archéologie de Bruxelles, Annales* 2 (1887): 14-15, for an account of the 1666 sale.

The 1683 sale will be discussed further on.

5. Ibid.

6. John Vermoelen, "Notes Historiques sur David Teniers et sa famille," *Revue historique, nobiliare et bibliographique* 8 (1870-1871): 156.

7. Ibid., p. 158.

8. Napoléon de Pauw, "Les trois David Teniers et leurs homonymes," p. 312.

9. Vermoelen, "Notes Historiques," p. 151.

10. One possible explanation for the lack of a burial record exists. If David the Younger was buried in the Church of St. Jacques sur Coudenberg, there might not be a record of his burial since the records of burials for this church were destroyed in a fire in the Archives de la Ville de Bruxelles. The Coudenberg church itself was demolished in the last years of the eighteenth century. A second church was erected on the site, but the individuals who were buried in the church were reinterred at the cemetery of the city Cathedral of St. Gudule. P. Lefevre noted this event in "Apropos de la sépulture de David Teniers III," *Archives, Bibliothèques, et Musées de Belgique* 12 (1935): 31-33. He quotes the following source for the transferal of the corpses, Archives ecclésiastiques, f°6875, Archives générales du royaume, Brussels. While this document apparently did not mention David Teniers the Younger, this seems the likely disposition for his remains. If he had been buried at Perck with Isabelle de Fren, might not his tombstone remain as hers did? It seems more likely to us that he would have been buried along with his first wife, Anna Brueghel and his son David III in their parish church in Brussels.

11. L. G. Galesloot, "Un procès entre David Teniers et la corporation des peintres, batteurs d'or, et vitriers de Bruxelles," *Messager des sciences historiques* (1868): 271.

12. Ibid., pp. 266, 269-70.

13. There are a few other works that were painted in the 1670s of which we have records. For example, de Pauw noted a painting created to celebrate the wedding of David Teniers III, *La Mystification Nuptuaile*, from 1671. Its present whereabouts is unknown. There is also a *Terrestial Paradise* or *Adam and Eve* (Smith, No. 134), which is also lost. This last was engraved by Le Bas. For a description of the *Mystification Nuptuaile*, see de Pauw, "Les trois David Teniers," pp. 338-40. An *Adoration of the Magi* recently passed through the New York art trade. This work is signed and dated, 1674, but it appears to us to be a copy of another master. It is not especially typical of Teniers. It is reproduced in *Apollo*, December 1977 (Sotheby's sale, January 13, 1978).

14. These are discussed in greater detail in Chapter 4.

15. Cataloged under Guysaerts, #1006.

16. Marie Louise Hairs, *Les peintres flamands de fleurs au XVIIe siècle* (Brussels: Meddens 1965), pp. 233, 334.

17. Jan-Baptiste Descamps, *Vie des peintres flamands et hollandais* (1754; reprint ed., Marseilles: Barle, 1842), vol. 3, p. 8, seems to be the source for this. There is no documentary proof that Antoine Teniers commissioned the series of paintings, but it seems entirely possible.

18. There is a diminishing of baroque style in the late works of Rubens tending

towards a quieter, less coloristic style and technique. Professor Erik Larsen has noted similar changes towards rococo taking place in the late works of Anthony Van Dyck.

CHAPTER 4

1. Philippe-Felix Rombouts and Theodore van Lerius, *De Liggeren en andere historische Archiven van het Antwerpsche St. Lucas gilde* (1864-1876; reprint ed., Amsterdam: N. Israel, 1961), vol. 2, pp. 119, 124 (Milese); 153 (van Bolder); 191, 234 (de Froey).

2. Ibid., p. 167, 171-72.

3. Ibid., p. 234.

4. Ibid., p. 18.

5. Ibid., p. 76.

6. Ibid.

7. Grimaldi sale, Cadiz, 1912.

8. Rombouts and van Lerius, *De Liggeren*, p. 173.

9. Ibid., pp. 11-16.

10. Instances of collaborations between David the Younger and Jacques d'Arthois are not numerous. The University of Wurzburg owns an example, monogrammed DT. Waagen's catalog of paintings in nineteenth-century British collections noted two landscapes by Teniers and d'Arthois at Arundel Castle. *Galleries and Cabinets of Art in Great Britain* (London: Murray, 1857), vol. 3, p. 31.

11. A. Wauters, "David Teniers et son fils, le troisième du nom," *Société royale d'archéologie de Bruxelles, Annales* 2 (1897): 31-32.

12. *Apollo* 112 (November 1969): 90. Sold in the Munich art trade.

13. Wauters, "David Teniers et son fils," p. 32.

14. Teniers also collaborated twice with the flower painter Christian Luyckx. *A Garland*, dated 1650, is owned by the Lasienski Palace, Warsaw. Teniers, Luyckx, and Teniers's sometime follower, Nicolas van Verendael, painted a *Vase of Flowers Before a Kitchen* in Dresden, #1091. The work is not dated. For a discussion of these works see Hairs, pp. 219, 421, 230, and 395.

15. Franz Joseph Peter Van den Branden, *Geschiedenis der Antwerpsche Schilderschool* (Antwerp: Buschmann, 1878-1883), pp. 603-8.

16. J. Denucé, *The Antwerp Art Galleries: Inventories of the Art Collections in Antwerp in the 16th and 17th Centuries* (Antwerp, De Sikkel, 1932), p. 261.

17. Francine Claire Legrand, *Les peintres flamands du genre au XVIIe siècle,* (Brussels: Meddens, 1963), p. 178. This survey of followers of the major genrists is most useful although Legrand did not go into much detail on the styles of various minor masters. This is obviously needed in this study of the Teniers connoisseurship. A mere list of followers is not sufficient.

18. Ibid., p. 167. See also van den Branden, *Geschiedenis*, pp. 916-18.

19. Van den Branden, *Geschiedenis*, pp. 916-18.

20. Legrand, *Les peintres flamands*, p. 167. See also Leo van Puyvelde, "Guillaume van Herp; bon peintre et copiste de Rubens," *Zeitschrift fur Kunstgeschichte* 22 (1959): 46-48.

21. Van den Branden, *Geschiedenis*, pp. 1015-18.
22. Ibid., p. 1027.
23. J. Denucé, *Na Peter Pauwel Rubens; documenten uit den kunst-handel te Antwerpen in de XVIIe eeuw van Matthys Musson* (Antwerp: De Sikkel, 1949), pp. 261, 285, 294.
24. Van den Branden, *Geschiedenis*, pp. 1022-24.
25. Ibid.
26. Rombouts and van Lerius, *De Liggeren*, p. 278 and passim.
27. Van den Branden, *Geschiedenis*, pp. 1103-4.
28. Legrand, *Les peintres flamands*, p. 176.
29. Van den Branden, *Geschiedenis*, pp. 1187-88.
30. Legrand, *Les peintres flamands*, p. 186.
31. Van den Branden, *Geschiedenis*, pp. 1181, 1211.

CHAPTER 5

1. See Eugene Dutuit, *Manuel de l'Amateur d'Estampes* (Paris: Levy, 1885), vol. 3, pp. 418-31. Dutuit lists some thirty-five prints that he attributes to David the Younger.
2. This print is noted in Dutuit, *Manuel,* p. 431.
3. See Ibid., p. 147 for a discussion.
4. For a consideration of Le Bas's prints after Teniers and their number, see *Gazette des Beaux-Arts* 2 (1910): 275.
5. R. Portalis and H. Beraldi, *Les graveurs de XVIIIe siècle* (Paris: Morgand & Fatout, 1882), vol. 2.
6. See the catalog of the prints of the G. G. Hubbard Collection of Prints (Cambridge, Mass.: Harvard University Fogg Art Museum, 1905), p. 22.
7. For a discussion of Chenu's prints after Teniers see *Gazette des Beaux-Arts* 2 (1880): 303.
8. There is, for example, an engraving of David the Elder's *Peasant with a Pole* (Alte Pinakothek) from the 1838 *Liber Studiorum* of the English engraver, John Sell Cotman. Cotman engraved the painting in the collection of Darwin Turner as one by David the Younger.

Appendix:
Dating the <u>Gerusalemme Liberata</u> Series

David Teniers the Elder was always very eclectic as we have seen from his frankly imitative paintings in the style of his own son. It has always been assumed that the initial designs for the series of *Gerusalemme Liberata* were his, although they were obviously modified towards a more baroque style as he collaborated with his son in finishing the paintings. Until recently no one has been able to date the paintings with more certainty than to state that they were painted sometime between 1628 and 1630. This date was based on the age of David the Younger as he appeared in the paintings in the character of Rinaldo and on the fact that they were painted before he entered the Antwerp guild. I still maintain that this is an accurate date for these paintings, but we are now somewhat closer to proving that these were painted in the late 1620s. Moreover, something more of their stylistic inception has been learned.

It has recently been discovered that some of the paintings in the *Gerusalemme Liberata* series have a distinct resemblance to certain works by Rubens executed in the 1620s. Apparently David the Elder saw these and borrowed some of Rubens's details of costume and overall design from his *Emblem of Christ Appearing to Constantine*, Plate 46, and his *Battle of Constantine and Maxentius*. These were sketches prepared by Rubens between 1621 and 1622 for the use of weavers who were creating a series of tapestries of the *History of Constantine* for Louis XIII. The costumes in the Teniers paintings also resemble those in Rubens's *Decius Mus* series, as well.[1] David the Elder seems to have based the composition of *A Scene in Godfroy's Camp*, Plate 47, on Rubens's *Emblem of Christ Appearing to Constantine* tapestries. The painting of *Armida in Battle*, Plate 48, is taken well as a similar treatment of background elements of landscapes and cities.

David the Elder's borrowings went further in that he also based at least one of the battle scenes in the *Gerusalemme Liberata* series on the *History of Constantine* tapestries. The painting of *Armida in Battle*, Plate 48, is taken from Rubens's *Battle of Constantine and Maxentius*. These two paintings are rather complex, writhing groups of soldiers.

Jan-Albert Goris and Julius S. Held have reproduced and discussed both these Rubens sketches in their 1947 book, *Rubens in America,* but they did not note any correlation with the Teniers paintings. They have, however, provided the dating for the finished tapestries and the drawings. They also note a letter written to Rubens from his friend, the scholar Peiresc, dated December 1, 1622, in which Peiresc mentions the drawing of the *Battle of Constantine and Maxentius.* We are thus able to establish the fact that the paintings by the two Teniers were created after 1622 since they are quite obviously based in part on the Rubens tapestries and their preparatory studies. We may say then that the *Gerusalemme Liberata* paintings were definitely painted in the 1620s. Moreoever, this helps bolster our case for these paintings being considered as a collaboration.

I do not feel that David the Younger's obviously baroque stylistic modifications are entirely based on his father's borrowings from these Rubens studies. David the Younger was merely reflecting a more general modern trend in composition as he assisted in the production of these paintings. Probably he himself was not so much influenced by Rubens as his father was in this case. David the Younger was, after all, keeping up with the mainstream of the newer style.

1. For a discussion of these studies and the *Decius Mus* paintings, see Jan-Albert Goris and Julius S. Held, *Rubens in America,* N.Y.: Pantheon, 1947, p. 38. The tapestries may be seen in the collections of the Philadelphia Museum of Art, which owns a complete set as well as the sketch of the *Emblem of Christ Appearing to Constantine.* The works reproduced in *Rubens in America* seem to be preparatory studies for the later cartoons. David the Elder may have seen these as well as the cartoons and the tapestries. David the Elder may have also borrowed the figure of Peter the Hermit, which appears in the Tasso series paintings, from Rubens. A very similar elderly bearded figure appears in *The Interpretation of the Victim* (Liechtenstein Gallery, Vienna), in the *Decius Mus* series.

Bibliography

This is by no means a complete bibliography of the rather extensive literature on David Teniers the Younger. The reader is referred to the author's dissertation listed below, for a more extensive bibliography.

Bie, Cornelis De. *Het Gulden Cabinet van de edele-vry Schilderconst.* Antwerp: Myssens, 1662.

Branden, Franz Joseph Peter van den. *Geschiedenis der Antwerpsche Schilderschool.* Antwerp: Buschmann, 1878-1883.

Davidson, Jane P. "Religious and Mythological Paintings by David Teniers II." Ph.D. dissertation, University of Kansas, 1975.

Denucé, J. "Brieven en Documenten betreffende Jan Brueghel I en II." *Bronnen voor de Geschiedenis van de Vlaamsche Kunst* 3: 1-172.

_____. *Na Peter Pauwel Rubens; Documenten uit den kunsthandel te Antwerpen in de XVIIe eeuw van Matthys Musson.* Antwerp: De Sikkel, 1949.

_____. *The Antwerp Art Galleries: Inventories of the Art Collections in Antwerp in the 16th and 17th Centuries.* Antwerp: De Sikkel, 1932.

Descamps, Jean-Baptiste. *Vie des peintres flamands et hollandais.* 1754. Reprint. Vol. 3. Marseilles: Barle, 1842.

Dewert, J. "Origine Wallonne des Peintres Teniers." *Bulletin de la Commission royale d'histoire de Belgique* 80 (1911).

Dezailler d'Argenville, Antoine Joseph. *Abrégé de la vie des plus fameux peintres.* Vol. 3. 1762. Reprint. Geneva: Minkoff, 1972.

Dutuit, Eugene. *Manuel de l'Amateur d'Estampes.* Vol. 3. Paris: Levy, 1885.

Duverger, Erik. "Bronnen voor de geschiedenis van de artistiche betreffingen tussen Antwerpen en de voordelijke Nederlanden tussen 1632 en 1648." *Miscellanea Josef Duverger.* Gent: Vereniging vorr de Geschiedenis der Textualkunsten, n.d., vol. 1, pp. 336-73.

Duverger, Erik and Vlieghe, Hans. *David Teniers der Ältere.* Utrecht: Haentjens, Dekker, and Gumbert, 1971.

Dreher, Faith P. "Discussion: David Teniers II Again." *Art Bulletin* 59: 108-11.

Galesloot, L. G. "Un procès entre David Teniers et la corporation des peintres, batteurs d'or, et vitriers de Bruxelles." *Messager des sciences historiques* 3: 236-75.

Hairs, Marie Louise. *Les peintres flamands de fleurs aux XVIIe siècle.* Brussels: Meddens, 1965.

Houbraken, Arnold. *De Groote Schouburgh der Nederlandsche Konsts-childers en Schilderessen.* 1718-21. Reprint. Maastricht: Leiter-Uypels, 1943-44, 1953.

Lefevre, P. "Apropos de la sépulture de David Teniers III." *Archives, Bibliothèques, et Musées de Belgique* 12: 31-33.

Legrand, Francine Claire. *Les peintres flamands de genre au XVIIe siècle.* Brussels: Meddens, 1963.

Mariette, Pierre Jean. *Abecedario.* Vol. 5. Paris: J. B. Dumaulen, 1858-1859.

Pauw, Napoléon de. "Les trois peintres David Teniers et leurs homonymes." *Academie royale d'archéologie de Belgique, Annales* series 5. 50: 310-59.

Peyre, Roger de. *David Teniers Biographie Critique.* Paris: Laurens, 1910.

Piles, Roger de. *Abrégé de la vie des peintres.* 1669. Reprint. Hilde-sheim: Olms, 1979.

Rombouts, Phillipe-Felix, and van Lerius, Theodore. *De Liggeren en andere historische Archiven van het Antwerpsche St. Lucasgilde.* 1864-1876. Reprint. Vol. 2. Amsterdam: N. Israel, 1961.

Rooses, Max. *Geschiedenis der Antwerpsche Schilderschool.* Gent: Hoste, 1879.

Rosenberg, Adolf. *David Teniers der Jüngere; Künstler Monographien.* Vol. 8. Leipzig and Bielefeld: Knackfuss, 1898.

Sandrart, J. von. *Teutsche Academie der Bau-Bild-und-Mahlerey Kunste.* 1675. Reprint. Munich: A. P. Peltzer, 1925.

Schellenkens, Oscar. *Les Trois David Teniers Peintres.* Termonde: Grotjans-Willems, 1912.

Smith, John. *A Catalog Raisonée of the Works of the Most Eminent Dutch and Flemish Painters.* Vol. 3. London: Smith and Sons, 1831.

Speth-Holterhoff, W. *Les peintres flamands de cabinets d'amateurs au XVIIe siècle.* Brussels: Elsevier, 1957.

Simillion, Konstantin. "Levensschets van David Teniers den jonge." *De Vlaamsche School* 10: 173-88.

Terey, G. von. "David Teniers und der Samtbreughel." *Kunstchronik und Kunstmarkt* 47: 780-87.

Vermoelen, John. "Teniers le Jeune; sa vie ses oeuvres." Series of articles. *Journal des Beaux-Arts et de la Littérature.* (December 1864-April 1865).

————. "Notes Historiques sur David Teniers et sa famille." *Revue historique, nobiliaire, et bibliographique* 8: 145-61.

Vlieghe, Hans. "David Teniers II en het hof van aartshertog Leopold Wilhelm en Don Juan van Oostenrijk, 1647-1659." *Gentse Bijdragen tot de Kunstgeschiedenis* 19: 23-49.

————. "David Teniers II in het licht der geschrieven bronnen," *Rijksuniversitat Gent Doc. V Hooger Institut voor Geschiedenis en Oudheidkundige* (1959): 35 ff.

Index